Voodoo & Hoodoo

Voodoo and its variant among black Americans, hoodoo, are still practiced. These are the stories and secrets of the hoodooers, voodoo women, and root doctors who serve paying customers all over the country right now in small Southern towns and large Northern cities.

Here are the "recipes" they use to kill, to cause illness, to cause living creatures to enter a body, to attract a man or a woman, to keep a lover faithful, to avoid the law, and to win at the numbers. Here's how they use graveyard dust to cast powerful spells, and the uses they make of High John the Conqueror root, Luck-in-a-Hurry Incense, human finger bones, as well as Stop Evil Floor Wash, Van Van Oil and red flannel bag "hands" to work signs, uncross tricks and gain power over others.

A privileged survey of conjury in the American black subculture, *Voodoo & Hoodoo* traces the phenomenon from its African roots to its practice today.

OTHER BOOKS BY JIM HASKINS

SCOTT JOPLIN

DIARY OF A HARLEM SCHOOLTEACHER

WITCHCRAFT, MYSTICISM, AND MAGIC IN THE BLACK
  WORLD

PINCKNEY BENTON STEWART PINCHBACK

THE CREOLES OF COLOR OF NEW ORLEANS

THE COTTON CLUB

and many more

VOODOO & HOODOO

HOODOO

Their Tradition and Craft as Revealed by Actual Practitioners

Jim Haskins

ORIGINAL PUBLICATIONS
22 East Mall
Plainview, New York 11803

To the Memory of Grandma Hattie

ORIGINAL PUBLICATIONS
22 East Mall
Plainview, New York 11803

ISBN: 0-942272-18-8

§§§

Contents

About the Author

JIM HASKINS has been a member of the Graduate Faculty of Education at Manhattanville College and a Visiting Professor of Literature and Folklore at Indiana University. He is the author of the acclaimed *Diary of a Harlem Schoolteacher; Witchcraft, Mysticism, and Magic in the Black World; Doctor J.* and many other books. He writes frequently for *The New York Times Book Review.* Born in Alabama, Mr. Haskins divides his time between New York City and Gainesville, Florida.

§§§

Acknowledgements

I am grateful to all those sources, practitioners and nonpractitioners, who asked not to be identified, and I hope they feel I have done justice to them and to the art of voodoo and hoodoo in this book. Thanks also to the following persons, who assisted me in my research or provided additional information: Frank Hendricks and Joseph Bush, of the Dixie Drug Store, New Orleans, Charles M. Gandolfo of the Voodoo Museum, New Orleans, Claude O. Winston, Jr., Lynn Bynum, Judy Griffin, Mrs. Dora Harrison, Molly Horwitz, Joan Loykovitch, J. M. Stifle, and Susan Fener. Mary Ellen Arrington typed the manuscript drafts, and Kathy Benson was of invaluable help in the task of organization.

§§§

Introduction

As a child growing up in a small town in Alabama, I shared the experience of most southern-born black children as well as that of many northern black children whose families had recently migrated from, or maintained close ties with, the South. We were aware from an early age that there were more forces with which to contend than met the eye. A person's very neighbors, though outwardly friendly, might be plotting against him, "laying a trick" on him. But they didn't perform the actual trick themselves; they had neither the power nor the knowledge. Instead, they went to the local hoodoo doctor or root worker. The black community in my small town had several, all of whom were known to the blacks as well as to many of the whites in the area. They didn't look any different from the other old black people, but they did seem to have an inordinate number of visitors. Particularly on Sundays, when even most blacks didn't work, there was considerable coming and going at these old folks' houses; and it was also on Sundays when the cars with out-of-state license plates would pull up and park on the street out in front. These old people occupied positions of considerable respect in the community, for though they were known to lay tricks they were also known to take them off. At any rate, there was usually nothing personal in the matter. They were professionals; conjure was their job and no one could fault them for that.

My family were relatively well educated, and they expected me to be even better educated, but that didn't stop them from respecting some very traditional mystical and magical beliefs, beliefs that can be traced back to West Africa. Unlike Alex Haley, I was not fortunate enough to hear stories of "the African" in my past from the elders in my family. But I was fortunate enough to have Grandma Hattie. I suspect that it was partially out of deference to her that her sons and daughters paid at least lip service to a number of superstitions and mystical-magical beliefs.

Respect for the old people in my family was total and unconditional. The old black people I knew as a child did not and would not set much store by the relatively recent philosophy that children ought to be respected, too. Among my most vivid childhood memories is one of sitting on the front porch steps listening to my grandmother and the other adults as they rocked in their chairs and talked about grown-up things. From time to time my grandmother would spit on me. Naturally it was uncomfortable, but I never dared object; and for quite awhile I chose to remain under the barrage of her spittle, thinking she was unaware that I was in the way and not wishing to offend her by moving or going away. It took me the longest time to realize that I was spat at only at particular points of the conversation: when topics were discussed that I was not supposed to hear. Grandma never said a word; and because she didn't, neither did any of the other adults. I learned from experience when to leave the front porch steps—as soon as Grandma started spitting. Grandma Hattie died shortly before this book went to press. Neither she nor I ever mentioned how I learned which conversations I was not to listen to. For me to mention it would have been disrespectful.

It was Grandma Hattie who gave me my first knowledge of hoodoo. She was not a practitioner herself and possessed a healthy skepticism about certain methods and claims of the known practitioners. For instance, she told me that serious illnesses and injuries were the province of medical doctors, not root workers, though the hoodoo practitioners might prepare effective-looking salves and ointments. Sadly, too many people in the community went to the hoodoo doctors. I recall seeing legs with huge, festering sores. Their owners should have gone to regular doctors; instead, they trusted the hoodoo doctors, got gangrene, and lost their legs.

Nevertheless, Grandma Hattie had a certain respect for hoodoo and for the people who practiced it. We children were not to go near their houses, and if we happened to pass these people on the street we were not to make fun of them nor aggravate them in any way, for things happened to people who displeased them. I recall that there was a man in the neighborhood who threw a brick at a dog that belonged to a local male hoodoo doctor. Within a week that man began gagging and vomiting. Though taken to the hospital, he grew progressively weaker and finally died. Disbelievers said it was mere coincidence; the old people rocked in their chairs and smiled knowingly.

I was warned not to eat anything at the homes of known practitioners or at the homes of people who visited them. Much conjure was accomplished by the use of food. Grandma Hattie told me of a man who died and whose stomach, when examined, was found to be full of baby snakes. The story was that someone fed him snake eggs. Nor was I to go to the bathroom in strange houses. Later in this book you'll understand why.

At birth, I was given a Christian name and a middle name. Shortly thereafter, I was also given a "basket name," not to be confused with a nickname. Nicknames have no inherent connotations or power; a basket name does. Only one's family and closest friends know one's basket name, and they use it only around each other. Should a stranger or even a casual friend know that basket name, it could be used against the person. In black magic tradition, one's name symbolizes in a very real way one's person, and things can be done with that name to cause harm to the person. I am educated, somewhat worldly I like to think, and I do not subscribe to voodoo and hoodoo beliefs, but I would not think of revealing my "basket name" to just anyone, and certainly not here.

Growing up in Alabama, I had little idea that other children were not raised with the same beliefs and superstitions. When I went away to school and lived elsewhere, coming into greater contact with whites, my personal horizons expanded and I began to look at these beliefs and superstitions differently. At the same time, however, my contact with blacks from dissimilar backgrounds and disparate geographical areas caused me to realize that there is a certain universality about these beliefs and superstitions among American blacks. I was not the only one who had watched women sweep their houses and yards, not just for the sake of neatness, but to sweep away conjure, or eaten rice and black-eyed

peas cooked together on New Year's Day to bring
good luck in the coming year, or been told my finger
would rot if I pointed it at a grave, or regarded
mirrors with some suspicion because they were so
often used in conjure or were connected with
various now-forgotten superstitions, or heard the
pronouncement that hanging a nutmeg on a string
around a baby's neck would aid in teething. Whatever our geographical, social, economic or educa-
tional backgrounds, most of us black Americans
share either a direct experience or an orally handed
down knowledge of the black mystical-magical tradition. I found it exciting to learn of this mutual
exper ence, and over the years I casually began to
collect bits and pieces of this tradition—information
that I now share with you in this book.

This is not intended to be a scholarly document.
Some of the primary material in this book was
collected rather haphazardly—in places where I or
my friends happened to be, rather than in areas
notable for geographical or cultural significance—
before I decided to compile the results in book form.
My emphasis has been singularly on the potions,
tricks, hands, and the like, and on their historical
basis, with only secondary interest in the backgrounds and personalities of their practitioners. I
must also state at the outset that my interest in voodoo and hoodoo has never been so great that I have
had any inclination to become an initiate. I admire
those, like Zora Neale Hurston, who spent weeks,
even months, with practitioners, learning their secrets firsthand. But though I appreciate the following inside view:

At three o'clock, naked as I came into the world, I
was stretched face downwards with my navel to the

serpent and a pitcher of water at my head that my spirit might not wander in search of it, and began my three day search for the favor of the Great One.

I've always preferred to retain the amenities of the non-mystical-magical world, and do not ever intend to become a voodoo or hoodoo practitioner. Other than having achieved some renown in folklore circles, Hurston evidently did not benefit to any great extent from her inside intelligence; and if folklore purists brand me a dilettante for the way I have researched my subject, I don't mind.

The persons who were interviewed for this book were practitioners, individuals who had observed or knew some of the formulas and methods of practitioners, and a variety of others who are involved in some way with voodoo and hoodoo practice—among them the operators of a drug store in New Orleans that does a sizable business in spiritualist supplies and the proprietor of a Voodoo Museum in New Orleans. All the practitioners and most of the other sources were middle-aged or older. Sadly, most young blacks fail to appreciate the significance of this body of lore handed down from generation to generation, although the situation may be reversed in the future. Following the practice of folklorists who've chronicled oral testimonies, the interviewees are given aliases when referred to or quoted here. Some even requested that their towns not be identified, in which case I have placed them in or near the largest nearby towns, or have provided no identifying information at all. Once assured of anonymity, they were quite willing to share their secrets. As Mother W. in New Orleans explained, "Some people say if I tell how to do the spells I won't be able to do them anymore. But only God can take away the power I have, and He won't do it until he gets ready—long as I do it for good and help people. Used to be, though, that folks wouldn't share their spells 'til just before they died. Then they'd call a grandchild to their bedside and tell him how to do it. That way they knew the power would be carried on."

Given their willingness to share their spells, you may wonder why they would reject the chance for free publicity; but most of the practitioners I've observed fare quite well on word-of-mouth publicity. Besides, their business depends to a considerable extent on mystery. If prospective clients were to know beforehand Doctor X's formula for causing rheumatism they might a) attempt to work the trick themselves, or b) decide the formula is less complex or effective than some other method about which they've heard. Those practitioners willing to share their secrets did so first, after being assured anonymity and second, I suspect, while at times leaving out an ingredient, or not specifying a portion, or failing to include an accompanying chant or mystical pronouncement, thereby protecting their secrets even if they should inadvertently give their identities away.

Grandma Hattie always said they were a smart bunch of people.

"Detectives smashed a grave-robbing ring early today as they rounded up the last of five teenaged suspects accused of stealing the skulls of long-dead women. The macabre loot was worth an estimated $1,000 on the occult market and was headed for voodoo . . . rites, detectives said. . . .

"There was no connection made between the grave robbers and a grisly discovery in a Bronx apartment yesterday. Maintenance men who entered an unoccupied apartment . . . found an altar, a human skull, a goat's skull, dried blood, and feathers apparently used in voodoo rites. An investigation was ordered."

Voodoo & Hoodoo

Note

Some of the procedures and techniques reported here, if put into practice, would be dangerous to one's health and safety. The author and publisher warn you *not* to implement them.

I

The Roots in Africa

Somewhere in West Africa a tall, lean man dressed in a short loincloth and feathered hat, with horns and gourds and a belt around his waist, bracelets and anklets made of seeds, dances alone in a circle drawn in the dirt. Those spectators who have questions to ask make small offerings of coins or vegetables. Periodically the man stops dancing and answers the questions.

Somewhere in the southern United States a wizened old woman in a faded print housedress and black laced shoes, her thinning gray hair pulled into a small bun at the nape of her neck, bends over her kitchen table mixing High John the Conqueror root (once an actual root gathered in the field now sold commercially), lodestone (metal filings) and sassafras together. Nearby sits an anxious young woman who listens intently to the old woman's instructions about how to use the powder. She hands the old woman a $5 bill and departs.

What do these two people have in common? They are both practicing magic, and carrying on a centuries-old tradition. The man in witch doctor regalia works in the cradle of that tradition, close to its roots, and the old woman in the faded print housedress prepares her spells in a land and a time warp far removed from these roots. She may not even be aware that many of the sources of her potions and prescriptions originated in Africa, but it is unlikely that she would be practicing had her heritage not been African. The man would probably scoff at the woman's watered down and adulterated procedures, and at her comparatively minor role in the life of her community, but he would recognize similarities between her methods and his own and marvel, like his Afro-American distant cousins, at the tenacity of the black mystical-magical tradition.

The voodoo, hoodoo, and spiritualism being practiced today are far removed from their origins, just as the black American, no matter what hair- and dress-styles or names and rhetoric he affects, is far removed from his. Yet in order to understand the black magical subculture as it exists today, it is necessary to understand it as a survival of its traditions. Thus one must be aware of what those traditions are. Here, then, is an overview of the system that existed in West Africa at the time of the slave trade. Scholars continue their efforts to trace African customs directly to aspects of life and black psychology today. That's not the intent here. This overview will provide you with some background of voodoo and hoodoo and explain the context of its transmittal to the New World and its survival into twentieth century Western society.

One of the most distinctive characteristics of a primitive society is its world-view, its relationship to the universe. Unlike the more advanced technological man, the primitive man sees himself as an integral part of the universe. There is no such thing as alienation in primitive cultures, no word in their language to describe a sense of separation or differentiation from surrounding forces.

We modern, "civilized" individuals regard ourselves as separate from, and above, these forces, for in large measure we are able to control them. We can seed clouds and produce rain. We can move mountains from the paths of the highways we build. We can build mammoth dams and alter a river's flow that nature has dictated for millions of years. We can take a desert and make it bloom, tap the depths of the earth for oil. In the hot summers we use air conditioning to create an artificially cool environment; in the midst of our concrete cities we can plant small tropical rain forests. There are a few natural forces we have yet to bring under control—earthquakes are one. But though we cannot yet control earthquakes we are in the process of developing sophisticated earthquake-detecting machinery that will enable us to anticipate and prepare for them.

Once something comes under our control, it loses much of its importance to us. Most individuals in highly developed societies have little interest in the natural world around them. Few are aware, for example, of the properties of various rocks, of the ebb and flow of the tides. Many are only dimly aware of the changing seasons. "I was so busy, I missed spring" isn't an uncommon statement in our busy, technological society. Some of our separation from the forces of nature is not our individual responsibility but the fault of our civilization. Even the suburbanite is more likely to consider a sweet potato a supermarket commodity rather than a living thing sensitive to the changes in its environment and able to yield new life.

We tend not to see the things we control, just as we tend not to see the people we control. We are increasingly separate from other people—from our parents as well as our children, from our neighbors as well as our co-workers. And more and more we see ourselves not as cogs in the machine of nature but as separate, discrete entities placed on earth for some unknown reason to live a life for which it is impossible to find meaning, and finally to die, allowing for no continuance of our personality.

Not so in primitive societies. There the individual doesn't see himself as separate. Indeed, his very identity—another word for which there is rarely a translation in primitive languages—or, rather, his being, is defined in terms of the people and the world around him. His name is often derived from nature. He sees himself first as a member of a family, a clan, a tribe, a village. His livelihood, and sometimes his very life, depends on the natural world around him, on the droughts and floods, the rocks and trees, the changes of the seasons. The sweet potato, or yam, may be the staple of his diet; in a way, he is controlled by the yam, and he sees it not merely as an item to be cultivated and eaten but as imbued with power to affect his life. The river is not simply a provider of water or a boundary marker for the land, but a hard taskmaster that will dry up and refuse its abundant moisture or overflow and destroy the village crops.

The soil, the rocks and mountains, the trees, the rivers are all believed to be inhabited by spirits—spirits that never knew human form. They share spirit-space with the ghosts of departed ancestors. The latter continue to affect the lives of their offspring, positively or negatively, depending on how they were treated when alive. And they exercise as tangible an effect as do the spirits of natural phenomena. Air, then, is not merely oxygen and other gases as we know it, but an active invisible plane of existence inhabited by a plethora of beings, like busy molecules affecting the human existence in demonstrated ways. They interact with the living and the living interact with them. This interaction among all things, this view of the world as a force field, is the basis of the religion and the magic of a primitive society.

We have religion in our technological societies, and we have magic. But the two are not only separate and distinct from one another, they are also separate and distinct from our daily lives. Not so in primitive cultures, where religion and magic are deeply imbedded in nearly every aspect of daily life. The forces of the universe are always close at hand and always accessible, to be consulted when important steps are to be taken, to be appealed to when help is needed.

So it was in the West African cultures when European slave-trading ships reached the

shores of the African continent in search of
human cargo. These cultures were varied, to be
sure, but they shared the same basic religious
and magical beliefs and practices born of
similar geography and living conditions. Such
similarities would prove important to the co-
hesiveness of the slaves when they reached the
New World and to the subsequent development
of their unique subcultures in the New World.

Currents and tides and distance dictated the
main slave-gathering areas. The northernmost
point was generally Gambia and from there
southward through Senegal, Mali, Sierra Leone,
Liberia, Ghana (formerly the Gold Coast),
Dahomey, Nigeria, the Cameroons, Zaire (formerly the Congo), and Angola. Certainly it is
possible that some slaves were brought in from
the deep interior or from areas farther south,
but the majority of slaves would naturally have
been taken from the coastal areas, which were
the most accessible. By the time the slave trade
was in full operation, different European countries had established dominion over the slave
market in various sections of the West African
coast. Senegal, the coast of Dahomey, the Cameroons, and parts of the Congo region were
primarily the domain of the French. Gambia,
the Gold Coast, and the area now known as
Nigeria were dominated by the English. The
Dutch operated in parts of the Gold Coast,
Nigeria and the Congo, while the Portugese
controlled Angola and parts of the Congo.
These areas included a large number of different tribes, but they were all related by language: all were of the Kwa- and Bantu-speaking
peoples; and, as mentioned earlier, they shared
similar religious and magical beliefs.

The basic West African religious system was pyramidal, with the supreme being at its apex, the center of divine power. From that point, in descending order and in descending power were the lesser deities. Immediately beneath the supreme being were the deities that did the bidding of the creator, and whose responsibility was the smooth operation of the world of man and nature. They manifested themselves as the gods of rivers and mountains, fire and iron, of lightning and epidemics, of war and peace. Beneath these deities were the ancestor spirits. Their duty was to see that their earthbound ancestors carried out the moral precepts handed down to them. The bottom of the pyramid was inhabited by the leaders of the social group, of the family or tribe or clan.

Closely associated with the deities, but not included in the basic hierarchy, were certain other forces. One was fate. West Africans believed that the destiny of each man, everything that happened in his life, was predetermined. In this belief they differed little from most other peoples, whether Indo-European or Asiatic. They, too, had methods to divine fate. The Europeans had the Tarot, the Chinese, the I Ching. In the I Ching, six bamboo sticks are thrown and the resultant hexagram is associated with a particular message. West African divination was also based on a system of combinations, this time arrived at by throwing a set number of seeds, each combination also associated with a particular message or parable.

The difference between the African concept of fate and that of other cultures was that in the African belief fate could be subverted with the aid of another force—the divine trickster. Actually, the divine trickster was a concept rather than a single deity, for it could take several forms. Some tribes envisaged the lesser deities organized into a series of family groupings that paralleled those of men. In these the divine trickster was often seen as the youngest child of one of the deities. One of the child's duties was to carry messages from the deity to the various divine families—messages that foretold what was in store for man. As a trickster, he could be persuaded by man to alter the orders he carried, to deliver a message different from that with which he had been entrusted. Thus, if some unhappy fate were in store for a man who was a serious worshipper, he could persuade the trickster to substitute a better one. The divine trickster could also be the ancestor who had most recently died. New to the afterworld and therefore supposedly closer to the living, he might be expected to be more in sympathy with their problems. The trickster might be an acknowledged deity in his own right whose particular responsibilities, such as a messenger of the gods, might make him suitable.

There was considerable interaction between man and these various forces and deities. When the aid of ancestors was invoked, the living were generally able to interact with them without the help of intermediaries. These practices were ritualized and a matter of custom.

The African's relationship with his ancestors was not, as has been misinterpreted by Westerners, "ancestor-worship"; ancestors were not revered as gods. Rather than revered, they were esteemed, at least those who, during their earthly lives, merited it. A man who lived a no-account life was not esteemed after death. A great warrior, an exceptionally virtuous person, or a wise leader was.

The demonstrated regard for the ancestor began at death with elaborate funeral rites. Extended and costly rituals were the best way the family could assure itself of the good will of the ancestor—a belief that continued in the New World. In succeeding years the ancestor was honored and kept ever-present in the daily life of the family. When meals were served, a portion was set out for him. During prayer, remarks were addressed to him, and at periodic intervals special festivals were held in his honor. Though this might appear to be ancestor worship, there was little sense of self-denigration among the living with respect to their ancestors. Ancestors were seen as part of the family, a plane of existence removed, perhaps, but not dead. An ancestor was not dead until he was no longer remembered by the living. But given the elaborate customs of oral history, that was highly unlikely to happen. There was no clear demarcation between life and death; rather, the living, the dead and the not-yet-born were all seen as part of the family and, in a broader sense, of the community. Thus the old were treated with honor and esteem, for in a sense they were almost-ancestors.

The ancestors retained a stake in the well-being of the family; they'd led a successful earthly existence and were willing to advise and help those who came after them. They came to the living in dreams, responded to requests for help from their descendants, and caused their own spirits to be reborn in the children of the family. Only if they were angered by lack of sufficient esteem did they refuse to help. The worst thing a family could do, for example, was to sell tribal ancestral lands, for the ancestors were the spiritual title holders of these lands. In such cases the family faced certain ruin; no amount of honor rendered could restore them to the good graces of the ancestors, and little help could be offered by outside intermediaries.

Africans had a different relationship with the higher deities. It was neither as intimate nor as informal, nor could they count on the benevolence of the gods in exchange for their worship. An individual could not successfully address one of these gods directly; rather, he needed the help of an intermediary. Thus the priest was an important figure in African religion. Only the priest or priestess knew the proper rites and ceremonies attendant to the sacrifice, one of the most important activities in West African religion. Sacrifices were offered for four major purposes: to pacify or appease deities; to prevent disaster or misfortune; to purify, usually an individual; and to offer a substitute for that which the deity desired. Hundreds, if not thousands, of sacrifices were offered each day for all manner of reasons: at puberty, marriage, birth, and death ceremonies, to ensure a good harvest, to counteract failure in business or agriculture, to drive away illness, to help ensure success in war. Each sacrifice was conducted in a traditionally prescribed manner with traditionally prescribed objects and activities. Sacrificial objects could include animals or fowl, the first fruits of the harvest, or the area's most valuable commodity. They could also include human beings. Ritual prescriptions might include the use of particular colors or the performance of a task a specified number of times. In each case only the priest or priestess was qualified to conduct the sacrifice.

An intermediary, or priest, was also necessary in the supreme experience in West African religion: possession. Like that phenomenon in European culture, possession in African religion involved the deity's assumption of the individual's identity and consciousness. For the duration of the experience, the subject retained no will of his own and indeed knew nothing of what he did while under the spell. Unlike the experience of possession in European cultures, which nearly always occurred when the individual was alone, possession by a deity in Africa most commonly occurred during some sort of ritual or celebration. At these rites a follower of the god was moved, by the rhythm of clapping or drum-beating or by singing, to allow his identity to be subsumed by the deity. There were definite and traditionally prescribed rules governing how he was to behave while possessed, how he was to be controlled by the person in authority at the ceremony, and how he was to be cared for when his possession was over.

Thus, although the African was in many ways on intimate terms with his religion, he looked to intermediaries to lead him in its practice. The same was true in related areas of African life and belief, notably magic.

In Africa the lines between religion and

magic were indistinct, the practice of one frequently entering the domain of the other. In Europe magical practices were not regarded as affecting God. The practice of magic, in fact, was seen as antithetical to religion. By contrast Africans believed that magic and witchcraft could very powerfully affect their spirits and their gods, not to mention each other.

The African viewed life essentially as a battle in which he was constantly in danger. Though he might enjoy an excellent relationship with the spirits of his ancestors, that didn't ensure protection against the evil designs of his neighbors. The attribute he regarded as most valuable—his vitality, or life-force—was open to all manner of attack from a variety of hostile forces in his environment. We, on the other hand, may be aware that our vitality is threatened by things in our environment, by food additives or emotional stresses that create a favorable climate for various cancers, for example, but we do not ascribe evil intentions to the creators of saccharine or red dye No. 2. If we feel tired all the time, we look to our own lifestyle to find the cause—taking into account diet, exercise, and psychological stresses that may produce psychosomatic illness—things that are not considered unnatural. The African who felt constantly tired, however, saw the state as highly unnatural and attributable to the evil machinations either of the spirits or of the people around him.

To counteract these evil forces, he had to seek the advice of an intermediary, in this case a medicine man. Next to the priests, medicine men were the most important people in the African community. Products of years of training in the properties of various herbs and roots, they were not merely the primitive counterparts of modern medical doctors. Just as the lines were blurred between African religion and African magic, so were the functions of the priest and the medicine man overlapping. Besides prescribing potions, the medicine man also knew the methods to invoke magic for healing purposes. Not only herbal mixtures, but taboos and sacrifices, chants and incantations were often necessary to exorcise illness, and the medicine man was far more knowledgeable and qualified in these matters than was the priest.

In the African belief system, for every good there was a corresponding evil, for every left there was a right, for every up, a down, and so on. Similar in some ways to the oriental concept of yin and yang, this belief in opposites was basic to both African religion and African magic. In the temporal world, then, the medicine man had his counterpart in the sorcerer.

The attitude toward the sorcerer in West African society was somewhat ambivalent. In times of peace and prosperity, he was likely to be killed or banished if identified, for he was seen as destructive and threatening to the society's structures. In times of warfare or other threatening situations, a tribe's sorcerer would be one of the powers relied on to help assure the tribe's safety and victory. Under such circumstances the evil force could be of benefit. He was then a "necessary evil." Trained as carefully as the medicine man and equally as knowledgeable as his "good" counterpart in the properties of herbs and roots and in the mystical forces of certain practices and chants, his task was to attack the vitality of man by the casting of spells and by poisoning.

There were hierarchies of both medicine men and sorcerers. Some possessed more power than others, but there were few whose work could not be undone. To lift the spell of a sorcerer, one needed to find a more powerful medicine man. To counteract the protection offered by a medicine man, a more powerful sorcerer had to be found.

Thus, though a man was constantly subject to evil forces, he was not actually at their mercy. He retained a modicum of control in that there was always an opposite and counteractive force to be employed, as long as one who knew how to invoke such a force could be found. The African often felt much more secure in his ability to manage his temporal existence than does twentieth century technological man.

Within the basic West African belief system there were regional and tribal differences which would affect slave life in the New World. Of the various West African peoples, the Fon-speaking people of Dahomey have been among the most carefully studied.

The supreme being recognized as the creator of all things by Dahomeans was called Nana Buluku. However, though acknowledged, he was not directly worshipped, being considered far above and unconcerned with the affairs of man. Below Nana Buluku, and seen as more accessible to man, were his two descendants, Mawu and Lisa. (In Dahomean theology, the gods were grouped in the same manner as men in terms of hierarchy and familial-type relationships. Just as man had descendants, so too did the gods.) Representing masculine and feminine, moon and sun, age and youth, they were viewed as linked together. Though Dahomeans rarely made representations of their deities, when Mawu and Lisa were represented they were depicted as a Janus-like figure. Dahomeans had a name for the interaction of these two deities and the opposites they represented. *Da*, meaning force or power, was represented as a serpent, and the serpent was the dominant Dahomean religious symbol.

Below Mawu and Lisa were the lesser deities, offspring of the twin deities and identified by the collective term *vodu*, a term that could also be used to refer to sacred objects representing, or associated with, the gods. These vodu controlled the day-to-day activities of man and were the gods of rivers, of war, of fire, and so on. Represented by objects such as stones, plants and bits of iron, they were worshipped with music and dance. Of these, the most frequently and universally worshipped was Legba. Originally the god who guarded entrances, he later became the god of the crossroads and the one who opened the way for other gods to be present at tribal rituals. He was the Dahomean divine trickster, the messenger of the gods who could be prevailed upon to alter messages and change fates.

In addition to the deities who were descendants of Mawu and Lisa, there were a number of others who had been adopted into the Dahomean pantheon. These were the gods of conquered peoples. The Dahomeans were a very warlike people, whose chief enemies were the Western Yoruba. Annually in the eighteenth century, for example, they engaged in forays against neighboring tribes, enslaving them and imposing their culture on them. However, they often spared from slavery the priests of the conquered tribes so as not to anger unduly the tribes' gods. The conquered peoples, in like manner, were not particularly resistant to accepting the Dahomean gods. After all, these gods had helped the Dahomeans to be victorious; clearly, they must be very powerful gods, and perhaps accepting and worshipping them would cause the worshippers to be more powerful too.

The bottom level of the Dahomean pantheon was occupied by the ancestor spirits, who were themselves deified and who enjoyed a close relationship with the gods.

Another of the dominant cultures of West Africa was that of the Yoruba. They, too, believed in a supreme being who was far removed from the affairs of men. Called Olódūmare or Olorun, this supreme being delegated control over the affairs of men to lesser deities, who were arranged in a hierarchy and known by the collective name orishas. There were no twin deities just beneath the supreme being as among Dahomeans. The most important of the lesser deities was Orunmila, god of wisdom. Next was Ogun, the god of steel and iron. Beneath him was Shango, god of lightning and thunder, and so on. The trickster in the Yoruba belief system was called Esu or Eshu, although in areas that had been conquered by Dahomeans, he had been amalgamated with the Dahomean trickster, Legba, and was called Eshu-Elegba. Beneath these lesser deities were the ancestors, who were deified by the Yoruba as by the Dahomeans.

Less is known about the religion of the Akan peoples, notably the Ashanti. However, it appears that their conception of the supreme being may have been closer to the western conception in that there seem to have been three levels of deity similar to the Christian Father, Son, and Holy Ghost. Also, only the Ashanti erected temples to their gods. The name of the Ashanti supreme being was Nyame or Onyame, who, like the supreme beings of other peoples, was far removed and uninvolved with the daily concerns of man. Nyankopon was closer and addressable by man, as was Asase Yan, the god of earth. Below these deities, or levels of the same deity, were the lesser gods, called *abosom*, gods of rivers, mountains, etc. Ancestors were revered but not actually deified.

This was the general mystical-magical belief system that Europeans encountered at the beginning of the slave trading era. It was not, however, recognized as a system, but as an extremely primitive hodgepodge of naive beliefs and practices that soon became labeled simply and incorrectly "fetishism" or "animism."

According to Geoffrey Parrinder, author of *West African Religion,* the Portuguese, the first

European traders to do business along the western coast of Africa, were also the first to apply the term fetishism to describe the religions they encountered:

They called the African charms and cult objects *"feitico,"* with the meaning of magical, like the talismans they themselves wore, the word deriving from the Latin *"factitius,"* for a thing of art. But anything could be called "fetish" and the first reference to it in English says that "the chief fetiche is the snake," which is hardly a magical object made by art.

In ensuing decades, even centuries, the identification of African religion as "fetishism" became more and more deeply entrenched. The term was improperly applied, of course, but if it *were* to be applied to the African custom of carrying amulets, or making sacrifices, or creating sacred images, then it would have to be applied to the religious-magical customs of every European culture as well. As Parrinder reminds us, the Portuguese wore talismans. If the Yoruba invoked Ogun, god of iron and steel, by kissing a piece of iron, that is a practice not unfamiliar in Christianity. Nor was sacrifice peculiar to African mystical-magical beliefs. As a student of Ashanti culture, R.S. Rattray once reflected:

It would be as logical to speak in these terms of the religion of ancient Greece and Rome, pulling down from their high places the Olympian Deities ... and branding ... the great thinkers of old, e.g., Plato and

Socrates as fetish worshippers. "I owe a cock to Aesculapius," said the latter almost with his last breath, and this pious injunction to his friend would be understood by every old Ashanti today.

Animism is another term frequently used then and much later to characterize the religion of West Africa. Meaning a belief that spiritual beings inhabit natural things, it may be considered a description of one aspect of the African belief system. One aspect, however, is not the whole, and the term, when used in the all-encompassing and frequently derogatory manner in which it is generally applied to West Africa, fosters more misconceptions than it explains beliefs. To describe West African religious beliefs as animism is to ascribe impersonality to the inhabiting spirits, who, in reality, are quite personal. That sort of description also tends to confine the spirit to the natural object it inhabits, a rock for example, when the spirit, although it may have an affinity to a particular natural object, is believed to be found everywhere. Further, it confines the African deities to the temporal plane, the practical level, and discounts the philosophical aspects of the West African belief system, which universally appears to have acknowledged the presence of a supreme being, creator of all things.

There were some observers and serious students of African religion who recognized that the popular Western judgements were false and misleading. In his Hibbert Lectures of 1878, Professor Max Mueller had this to say:

I maintain ... that the Negro is capable of higher ideas than the worship of rocks and stones and that many tribes who believe in fetishes cherish at the same time very pure, very exalted, very true sentiments of Deity. Only we must have eyes to see, eyes that can see what is perfect without dwelling too much on what is imperfect.... Religion is everywhere an aspiration rather than a fulfillment; and I claim no more for the religion of the Negro than for our own, when I say that it should be judged not by what it appears to be, but by what it is—nay not only by what it is but by what it can be and by what it has been in its most gifted votaries.

Men like Mueller were in a minority in those days, and they were rarer still in the early days of the slave trade.

The stage now has been set for the arrival of the African slaves in the New World, the beliefs they brought with them, and the attitude toward those beliefs that they encountered. No matter from which area or tribe in Africa they were taken, no matter to which region or country in the New World they were brought, they faced a culture clash calculated to uproot or seriously alter their most deeply-held beliefs. Yet, somehow, many of these beliefs have survived in one form or another to this day, in the Southern states, in the Caribbean, in the West Indies, and even in some areas of the northern states. How and why they have survived has depended to a considerable extent on a variety of factors, but the most important is cultural. The dominant cultures in the areas to which the West Africans were transplanted as slaves have proved the determining factor not only in the survival of African religious and magical practices and beliefs but in the survival of Africanisms in general.

§§§ II

Culture Clash and Accommodation in the New World

Gullah Jack (one of the leaders in Denmark Vesey's Insurrection in South Carolina in 1822) was regarded as a sorcerer ... He was not only considered invulnerable, but that he could make others so by his charms (consisting chiefly of a crab's claw to be placed in the mouth); and that he could and certainly would provide all his followers with arms.

—Newbell Puckett, 1926

By 1822 slaves had been in North America nearly one hundred fifty years; yet here we find an "African sorcerer" fomenting a revolt in South Carolina. Not much is known about Gullah Jack, but it is unlikely that he was born and bred in the States. New slaves were continuously being brought to North America from Africa—smuggled in after the African slave trade was prohibited—and from the West Indies and Latin America. From all accounts, these were the slaves who helped most to keep alive in North America the magical traditions of Africa. How many slave insurrections were led by sorcerers, or men who claimed to be sorcerers, is not known. What is known is that the majority of uprisings took place in those areas where geographical isolation and large numbers of slaves made it possible for them to give vent to their grievances by way of organized revolt. Others did not enjoy such circumstances, and it will be seen that the nature of the various political, social and geographic environments would have important bearing on how much of their original culture the slaves in the New World were able to retain.

The overwhelming fact of the African's experience in the New World was the brutal severing of nearly every element basic to his identity. He was separated from his family, from his village, from his tribe, from his language, from his religion, from his entire socioeconomic experience—not to mention the separation from his land. The loss of freedom cannot be overlooked, but in the context of the African's basic identity it is not the major factor. Slavery was not alien to the African—the practice was common among the tribes before European and Arab slave traders descended. But a slave in Africa had some knowledge and familiarity with the beliefs, language, and customs of his captors. Their gods might have different names but they were similar in conception; their societal structures were not alien, nor were their economic concepts. There were solid bases for adaptation and accommodation that did not exist in the New World experience.

Basic to the identity-shattering New World experience was the feeling of total hopelessness. The slaves knew they would never see their homes again. Intra-African slavery involved no geographical gap so huge as the great water, no time passage as long as the months spent crossing the Atlantic. The awareness that there was no possible way to return home overwhelmed the other indignities and sources of strangeness for a time. But these soon assumed their perspective.

The slaves had difficulty communicating with one another, for they represented a variety of tribes and dialects. They were further discouraged from developing means of communication by the traders, who understandably feared that communication would lead to cooperation, which in turn would lead to revolt. They were shackled, roughly treated, poorly fed, denied even a semblance of humanity, transferred from one ship to another, moved overland like so many cattle in wagons, placed on auction blocks in front of crowds of leering, greedy people, until at last they reached their destination: a huge plantation in Jamaica or Haiti, a small farm in the South, or a town in New England. There, settled at least for a time, they had the opportunity to acclimate themselves to their new surroundings.

Slaves on large, absentee-owner plantations had considerably greater opportunity to regroup and reinstall some of their traditions and social organization. Slaves on smaller farms or in towns were too frequently under the watchful eye of whites and usually too few in number successfully to accomplish such cultural reorganization. Accommodation to white customs occurred much more quickly under those conditions and by the second or third generation much of the African heritage had been forgotten. Simple geography and population considerations aside, the most important factor in the slaves' new environment was the cultural tradition of that environment. Whether it was Latin-Catholic or English-Protestant deeply affected the possibilities for continuation, albeit in altered form, of the African heritage.

The Latin countries had considerably more prior experience with slavery than did England, and over the centuries a body of law concerning slaves had been created. Spain, for example, had an elaborate slave code as part of its basic legal system developed in the thirteenth century; and as the mother country exercised strict control over its colonies, that body of law, including the slave code, was applied as strictly in the Spanish areas of the New World as it was in Spain. Under the slave code, slaves were established as human beings and given certain rights, among them the right to buy their freedom, to marry and to have children. The English, on the other hand, had no prior slave tradition and consequently no laws pertaining to the slaves. Having no legal identity, the slave also had no rights. His personhood was not guaranteed; indeed, when laws dealing with him began to be passed he was treated as property. Then too, the English colonies were basically self-governing. Although theoretically answering to the Crown, they had considerable freedom to pass their own laws and establish their own customs, which came under review primarily when they affected the income or openly brooked the authority of the Crown. There is little historic evidence that the mother country ever had much interest in how the

slaves in the colonies were treated. Had
England been Catholic, the situation would
probably have been considerably different.

The Latin governments, as governmental-
legal systems, were no more moral or human-
itarian than the English. But the Latin
governments answered to the Church; the English Crown did not. Through the British separation of church and state, the Church lost
much of its power, and in the colonial period it
had considerably less power in the overseas
territories than it did at home. Fiercely posses-
sive of their right of self-government, the colo-
nists subsumed the Church to their own
interests, and their own interests did not include elevating the slave above the status of
property.

There were harsh and brutal Latin slave
owners, and benevolent English ones. The gov-
ernmental influences outlined here were neither uniform nor universal throughout their
respective dominions. In general, however,
slaves under the Latin system were acknowledged as persons; slaves under the English
system were classified as property. So the
former were subject to considerably more religious proselytism. As it happens, the Roman
Catholic Church was by nature far more acceptable to the slaves than the other. Coinci-
dentally, the Fon people of Dahomey and
Yoruba, who were most numerous in the Latin
territories, were also the slaves whose religion
was characterized by a highly developed
pantheon.

The Catholic Church had a pantheon of its
own. Its Virgin and its saints were understand-

able to Africans whose religious structure and traditions included lesser but important deities who were, like the saints, honored with festivals and rituals and prayed to for help in day-to-day living. Christianity even included a Devil, a spirit with whom the Africans could easily find parallels. The Catholic religion was also highly ritualistic; its Holy Communion, holy days, and its services could correspond in the African's mind to his own rituals, its rosary beads and icons to his talismans. And not only did the equation exist, it was encouraged. The Church decreed missionary work among the slaves. Conversion to Catholicism, ideally in its pure form, was wanted, but given the "primitive" and "heathenish" background of the slaves, certain adulterations of the practice of the faith were overlooked in the process of bringing new souls to God. Then too, many slave owners tended to carry out the letter rather than the spirit of the Church's directives, particularly in the French-held territories. As a group the French were the harshest slavers among the Latins. Slaves in Haiti, for example, were often herded into a church with whips and ordered to kneel, whereupon they were baptized en masse. Then they were herded back out to work, now officially converts to Christianity. In many areas it was possible for the slaves to be members of the Church while at the same time continuing essentially African modes of worship. As Melville Herskovits put it, "What seem to be far-reaching contradictions are reconciled without apparent difficulty, for the pagan spirit believed to control a given manifestation of the universe is merely identified with a given saint, and unless missionary pressure places the African spirit under a ban and removes the prestige it would normally receive as a functioning entity, no demoralization results."

There was no concept of betrayal inherent in adopting new gods in the African tradition. More than individual deities themselves, power was revered; and simply stated, the Africans worshipped what worked, or whoever was effective. Since the white masters were clearly powerful, it followed that one would do well to acknowledge their gods. Thus in Haiti, for example, where many slaves were of Dahomean heritage, the Dahomean serpent-deity Da was identified with Saint Patrick. The Dahomean Legba, guard of entrances and god of the crossroads, was identified with Saint Peter, keeper of the keys.

The slaves did not make such correspondence willy-nilly, or individually. They relied in the New World, as they had at home, on intermediaries. There were priests among those taken from Africa; and though at first they were probably as confused and helpless as their fellow slaves, they gradually established small bases for the continuation of their religious practices. Though the slaves themselves might not be able to go back across the ocean to Africa, no earthly barriers inhibited the spirits. Large bodies of water in the New World could be under the domain of the spirits who inhabited the waters of Africa. The priests are the ones who identified deities in the African pantheon with Catholic saints and who led the ceremonies in the worship of these deities. But

the priests were operating at a serious disad-
vantage, for they were inextricably identified
with the African cultural establishment, so to
speak. Their influence depended on kinship ties
and religious institutions that did not exist in
the New World and more importantly on a
basis of freedom and self-determination that
did not exist there either. As an entity separate
from the medicine man and the sorcerer, the
priest would gradually disappear.

Medicine men and sorcerers, too, were
brought to the New World as slaves. Both were
far more successful in plying their respective
crafts than were the priests. The medicine men
found in their new homes flora whose properties were similar to the African plants from
which they made or extracted their medicines.
This was particularly true in the Caribbean
islands, whose climate was tropical like that of
the West Coast of Africa. The sorcerers found
their renewal in the slavery-induced confusion
and disorientation among the Africans in the
New World. Under such conditions, those people who were hated and feared in Africa
became more acceptable and more powerful in
the slave community. Wisely, in Latin-held
areas they couched their activities in the guise
of the religious traditions that the slaves were
able to adapt to Catholicism. They and the
priests, who knew the techniques of sorcery
and used them to gain greater acceptability
among the other slaves themselves, gradually
blended into one. After a few generations, then,
the distinctions between the two once radically
different professions blurred. Out of this blur-
ring came voodoo, a term that can be related to

the Dahomean word for spirit, *vodun*, and to the more generalized West African *juju*, which is best translated to mean conjure. It became a fairly systematized body of mystical-magical practice and lore, the basis for the system being the amalgamation of European religion and African religion and magic, an amalgamation made possible by the nature of the Catholic religion and its philosophy, backed by action, of proselytism.

A different situation existed in the Protestant areas of the New World. Though the Church of England periodically sent out pious directives urging masters to convert their slaves to Christianity, it had no power comparable to that of the Church in the Latin territories. Not only did the slave masters in English colonies not feel constrained to obey the church directives, they firmly disagreed with them. In the Protestant colonies, where slaves were regarded as property, there was as little impetus to convert the slaves as to convert one's mule. Even those good Christians who entertained the notion of converting their newly arrived Africans despaired at the evidences of fetishism and other manifestations of heathenism they perceived. And of course the slaves helped them quickly to wash their hands of further attempts to save heathen souls. The slaves simply expressed little interest in a religion that allowed for no pantheon and little ritual.

Another major factor was traditional British logic, which held that if slaves were to be allowed the practice of religion they would undoubtedly use their gatherings as a means to plan revolts and insubordination. The British slaveholding custom was to prevent large slave congregations, and the custom was not to be relaxed simply for the questionable goal of trying to convert a bunch of heathens who were not legitimate human beings anyway.

There were also priests among the slaves carried to the British territories, but their lot was even worse than that of their counterparts in the Latin areas. They had no opportunity to adapt traditional African beliefs and customs to the religion of the conquerors, for they had little or no access to that religion.

It was a situation ripe for the ascendancy of the sorcerer. Traditionally concerned with more temporal matters and historically most powerful in times of disorientation and confusion, the sorcerer found fertile ground among the slaves in the New World. Denied much opportunity to practice their religion, even in adulterated form, the slaves in the British areas turned increasingly to their magic. By tradition it had been practiced in secret and so proved quite adaptable to the situation in which the slaves found themselves.

The Akan peoples, the Ashanti and Fanti, were the most numerous among the slaves brought to British America, and as with the Yoruba and Dahomeans in the Latin-held areas, it was their culture that gradually assumed prominence among most of the slaves. Unlike the Yoruba and the Dahomeans, their religious traditions emphasized a strong ancestor cult. In a book on Jamaica published in 1843, a Baptist minister described the practices he encountered:

Superstition itself in its most disgusting form prevailed among them to a very great extent. Dark and

magical rites, numberless incantations, and barba-
rous customs were continually practiced, the principles of these were *obeahism*, myalism and fetishism;
and such was their influence on the general mind . . .
that they were accompanied by all the terrors that
the dread of a malignant being and fear of the
unknown evil could invest.

Fetishism, of course, was a European term,
coined originally by the Portuguese. But obeahism was of Akan origin, deriving from the Twi
word *obayifo:* literally, he who takes a child
away, and more generally, a witch or a sorcerer. The obeahman in Jamaica had been an
important member of the slave community
since at least the middle of the eighteenth
century. White planters blamed obeahmen for
fomenting the Rebellion of 1760 and introduced
a law against them. The proposed law read in
part: ". . . any negroes or other slaves who shall
pretend to any supernatural power and be
detected in making use of blood, feathers,
parrot's beak, dog's teeth, alligator's teeth, broken bottles, egg shells or any materials related
to the practice of witchcraft . . . shall upon
conviction . . . suffer Death or transportation."
The law was adjudged too harsh by the Crown
and royal sanction was withheld.

The word myalism can also be traced to the
Akan languages, specifically to the Twi *mia;* to
squeeze or to press, as in extracting medicines
from plants. In Jamaica the myal-man or
-woman was the herbalist, the New World
medicine man, as well as the person to whom
one turned for help in undoing the sorcery
practiced by the obeahman.

In Jamaica, as well as in other British-held New World territories in the Caribbean, then, the slaves' metaphysical urges, denied expression in religion, were translated mainly into magical beliefs and practices with few religious trappings, and because of the nature of Caribbean society, the absentee land-ownership and the preponderance of slaves in comparison with whites, they were able to develop such practices despite opposition by their masters.

The slaves in North America had less leeway. Romantic visions of the old South notwithstanding, North America boasted few huge plantations. The large farm with perhaps twenty to thirty slaves more closely approximates the norm, and thus most North American slaves were less isolated from supervision than those in Latin America and the Caribbean and less able to carry on their group traditions unobserved. Under such conditions, traditional practices and customs disappeared more quickly, the rapidity dependent on the size of the plantation or farm, the attitude of the slave owner, and the geographic isolation and nature of the slaves themselves. (A farm or plantation whose slaves included a priest or sorcerer, for example, was more likely to harbor traditional occult activity, albeit in secret.)

There is evidence, however—recall the description of Gullah Jack cited earlier—that in some areas of North America the sorcerer contributed to the fomenting of revolts just as in the Caribbean. And there were cases in which a relatively well acculturated slave population re-adopted traditional practices as a result of an influx of less acculturated blacks.

Indeed, the most widespread and exotic mystical-magical cult in the United States owes its existence primarily to the arrival of large numbers of blacks from Santo Domingo in the early nineteenth century.

A revolt by the slaves against the white French planter class began in Santo Domingo in 1791 and lasted for thirteen years until the rebels succeeded in founding the independent, black Republic of Haiti in 1804. Thousands of French fled the island, taking with them as many slaves as they could. Thousands of Santo Domingan free people of color escaped, too, for they identified closely with the whites and were similarly identified by the rebels. Many of these refugees sought shelter in Cuba, across the Windward Passage; but when Napoleon invaded Spain in 1809 they were forced by Spanish Cuba to leave. Some ten thousand of these refugees found their way to New Orleans, and their impact on the city and its environs was considerable.

The black refugees, free and slave, were steeped in the knowledge and practice of voodoo, and they had a new respect for its rites and traditions. After all, Toussaint L'Ouverture, leader of the revolution and Haiti's first dictator, had been a root doctor. Even though he was a staunch Roman Catholic, he and other leaders of the revolution insisted that it had been the mystical powers of the voodoo priests that had given the black fighters the strength to drive their enemies to the sea. The Santo Domingan refugees began holding their voodoo rites in New Orleans, and New Orleans blacks joined them in their rituals and practices.

Many aspects of these rites, as performed at that time, are now fairly common knowledge: the serpent-worship, sacrifice and the drinking of blood, black cats and dismembered chickens, wild group dances in Congo Square, evil spells with dolls and pins, and the suspected kidnapping and murdering of white children. What is not commonly known is that from the beginning of the organized practice of voodoo in New Orleans, whites could be found among the cultists.

The open practice of voodoo in New Orleans did not last long. In 1803 New Orleans became American territory through the Louisiana Purchase, and within less than two decades it was brought firmly under the control of United States laws. A rash of anti-voodoo sentiment and legal action occurred about 1820 and again in the late 1830s, when all dancing in Congo Square was forbidden. By 1850 the campaign had become so vicious that some New Orleans newspapers were actually defending the voodoos. But the legal system was not to be mollified, and voodoo was never again practiced as openly and publicly.

Still, the secret practices continued, many under the cloak of Catholicism. Marie Laveau (1794-1881) is credited with influencing this change. A quadroon who is also believed to have had some Indian blood, Marie was a free woman of color who began her working life as a hairdresser to wealthy whites and later served as a procuress. Her memory is so heavily surrounded with legend that it is difficult to know how much is myth and how much is fact, but she was undoubtedly a shrewd woman

with an excellent business sense. In an era
when the voodoos were disorganized and many
queens vied with each other for preeminence,
Marie decided to become the undisputed
Voodoo Queen and by the time she was thirty-
six she had achieved her goal. Some say it was
her powerful charms that did it; others, that she
disposed of her opposition by trickery and even
physical force (she would beat them until they
promised to serve her). Once established, she
made the practice of voodoo a commercial
venture, putting it firmly on a paying basis. She
also Romanized voodoo practice, adding to
traditional voodoo paraphernalia statues of
Catholic saints, prayers, incense, candles, and
holy water. She was herself revered almost as a
saint, and took advantage of this reverence.
Even after conclusive evidence was produced
that her daughter, also named Marie, had taken
her place and, indeed, impersonated her, the
legend persisted in some quarters that the
original Marie had approached immortality.
The tomb said to be that of Marie I, in St. Louis
Cemetery No. 1, has long been a mecca for
voodoo believers. Its marble walls are covered
with Xs made with pieces of red brick, and the
attached cup is rarely empty. "Draw the X,
place your hand over it, rub your foot three
times against the bottom, throw some silver
coins into the cup, and make your wish," says
Charles M. Gandolfo, owner of the Voodoo
Museum in New Orleans, explaining one of the
common rites performed at the tomb. The
Voodoo Museum is located at 739 Bourbon
Street, where it is said Marie's daughter, known
as Marie II, once lived and where, in the small

brick courtyard, she conducted secret voodoo ceremonies. A painting of Marie I and a photograph of Marie II are displayed at the Museum.

Because of the influence of Marie Laveau, Saint John the Baptist became the patron saint of voodoo in New Orleans. "St. John's Eve is the most important date of the year," says Gandolfo.

Various other saints were ascribed new powers—Saint Raymond for favors, Saint Rita for children, and the like—and a number of new saints, not recognized by the Catholic Church, were invented to meet needs not met by existing saints. One of these was Saint Marron (or Maron) who was worshipped as the patron saint of runaway slaves. Another was Saint Expédite. The French *expédite,* like the English *expedite,* means roughly, "to make easier," and Saint Expédite was the saint to pray to when you wanted to get something done in a hurry. So important was this saint to New Orleans blacks that he continues to be worshipped even today. There are statues of Saint Expédite in New Orleans and at least two Saint Expédite spiritualist temples.

Specifically non-Christian practices continued as well. Robert Tallant, author of *Voodoo in New Orleans,* interviewed a very old black man named Joe Goodness who recalled witnessing voodoo rites when he was a child around the turn of the century and who remembered stories his uncle had told him of voodoo practice in even earlier times:

In my day they didn't even drink blood, that I know of, but only ate things like gumbo and chicken and drank a lot of liquor. In my uncle's day they did worse things. They wore all kinds of *gris-gris* tied on their bodies—dolls made out of feathers and hair, skins of snakes and pieces of human bone. I heard people say hoodoos was cannibals and used to eat babies, but I don't believe that unless it was 'way back even before my uncle was alive. I guess it's changed a lot, just like it's different now from the way it was when I was a little boy.

Folklorists who studied voodoo practice in New Orleans at the turn of the century and in the era before World War II found considerable evidence of a thriving cult. Of these students of voodoo, Zora Neale Hurston is the most reliable. Though Ms. Hurston was not above coloring her reports if it suited her purpose, being black she had a greater understanding of the practive of voodoo among black people. She was a graduate of Barnard College, but she seems to have approached her field work with remarkably little bias, and a considerable amount of enthusiasm. Here are some of the recipes she gathered in New Orleans, as reported in a lengthy article in the *Journal of American Folk-Lore* in 1931. First, examples of evil conjure:

§§ ... take sand and throw on the floor. Write on paper the names of the people concerned, and throw it on the floor. Rub the paper back and forth with your foot (like cleaning a needle). Pick up all the sand along with the particles of paper. Take a large bottle of iodine. Make a box and mix the sand with iodine. Put two black candles in the sand—one on each side. That starts your work. It drowns the enemies of the person for whom you work . . .

§§ (To give suffering with heart). One sheep's heart, enough good whiskey in a jar to cover the heart. Split it and insert the name of the victim. Nine pins stuck inside slit, and nine needles to close slit. Take a piece of new twine and tie tightly about middle of heart. Mix gin with whiskey and pure alcohol, and place heart in jar, and cover with fluid. Take nine black candles and burn one each day for nine days. He will die of heart trouble.

§§ (To fix a landlord). Take a pop bottle, mark the landlord's name nine times on paper. Take gin, whiskey, rum and put it in the bottle with his name. Take two spoons of sugar and put in bottle with river water, cistern water, and well water. Shake well every day at twelve o'clock. Burn a whole box of green candles. Put the box with neck down behind the bed in the corner.

§§ (To make a fight). Take the parties' names nine times and cross. Put the names in bad vinegar (fighting vinegar), two pounds of gunpowder, one dollar of cayenne pepper, two dollars of mercury, one box of black candles, fifty cents of blue stone, sour wine, two pounds snuff, nine packs King Bee tobacco. Burn in a barrel for nine days. Go to the corner nearest the parties and throw some of this mixture diagonally, then cross the street and go up the block and cross and throw again, then pass the gate or step and spill some.

And here are some recipes for beneficial spells that Hurston gathered:

§§ (For luck). Mix Dragon's Blood [one of the popular names of the Herb-Robert] with powdered sugar and steel dust and incense—to be worn in shoe or pocket. First wash your face with rose water and Jockey Club (perfume) to give you a good front.

§§ (To remove bad luck). Two pounds of bird seed, three pounds of brown sugar, two boxes of cinnamon (powdered), two whole ginger cakes. Powder the ginger bread and mix everything together, and throw it all around the step and let the seeds grow and their luck will grow.

§§ (To stay on the job). Have an altar in the house and let your client bring five cents worth of pecans. Both of you get before the altar. You eat one first, then your client. Then you eat them at the same time. Put all the hulls back in the bag and let her carry them back to work and throw them where they won't be swept away, as in the grass, etc., and nothing can move her.

§§ (To make love charms). Take powdered angleworm dust mixed with love powder and ground John the Conqueror root. Place the above articles in a small bag with a string on each end of the bag so as to meet around the waist. This charm will make your lover or sweetheart come to you and stay.

As slavery became more institutionalized in other parts of North America, as more laws and codes, written and unwritten, appeared, as slave trading was outlawed and died out and new slaves were culled from the offspring of other slaves, as revolts subsided and blacks and whites became more accustomed to living in proximity to each other, greater attempts were made to bring Christianity to the slaves. The Methodist and Baptist churches engaged in missionary work among blacks and many were admitted to membership. The Baptist Church was particularly attractive to the slaves, for certain aspects of its practice were identifiable with African religious traditions.

In West Africa, river cults were among the most important religious groups. A major part of the worship of river spirits was a pilgrimage to some sacred body of water where the most ecstatic experience one could have was to be possessed by the river spirit and to fling oneself into the water. Water was also very important in the Baptist faith, whose name and chief practices centered around baptism by water. The rite of baptism was supposed to be accompanied by the revelation of God, and in some Baptist churches an experience much like possession did happen to certain worshippers. Another aspect of the Baptist Church recommending it to the slaves was its organization, which allowed considerable independence for its local churches. During slavery, blacks usually joined the white congregations and were relegated to separate services and separate seating areas. Rarely were they allowed churches of their own, for whites clearly recognized the danger in allowing blacks to congregate together unsupervised. After emancipation, however, one of the first steps the freedmen took to demonstate their independence was to leave the white churches and establish their own. Allowed autonomy by the national Baptist organization, Negro Baptist churches became well known for their unique forms of worship. As a new member to be baptized was immersed in a stream or a pond and as the spirit of God descended upon him, he was far more likely to be possessed than was his counterpart in a white Baptist congregation. Another African tradition which was introduced into the black Baptist Church was the rule that new members go through a period of initiation, called "mourning," before baptism, just as did the priests of the African water cults.

Still, the Protestant religions were not, on the whole, as adaptable to African religious traditions as was Catholicism, and though certain religious elements were incorporated into the slaves' magical practices, these elements primarily constituted an overlay and did not measurably alter the practices themselves.

Over the years, mostly outside the New Orleans area, these magical practices were subsumed under the general term *hoodoo,* the origin of which is not directly traceable to a particular tribe as is that of voodoo. By most accounts, hoodoo is derived from *juju,* meaning conjure, but some theorize it may also be an adulteration of the term *voodoo.*Whatever its origin, the term referred to that body of magical practices that characterized black life in most

of North America and was essentially inter-
changeable with terms used in British colonies
in other areas, notably obeah in Jamaica.

The forms of hoodoo found in North America
outside of Louisiana in the latter part of the
nineteenth century were reported quite extensively in folklore journals of the time, although
the quality of reportage varied. As an example
of the type of prejudice that colored the writing
of many white contributors to these periodi-
cals, here is an excerpt from an article by one
Julien A. Hall of Morotock, Virginia, that appeared in the *Journal of American Folk-Lore* in
1897:

The readers of the *Journal* are no doubt familiar
with many of the superstitions and beliefs of the
negro race in regard to "conjuring" and "tricking."
These beliefs were brought here from Africa by the
first comers and continue in full force to this day,
notwithstanding the negro is a freeman and living
amongst the white people in the United States of
America, who are probably as practical as any
human beings on earth . . .

The year before, the *Journal* had quoted
extensively from an article by Misses Herron
and A. M. Bacon that had appeared in the
*Southern Workman and Hampton School Re-
cord* for November and December 1895. Titled
"Conjuring and Conjure-Doctors in the Southern United States," the study was based on
compositions of students at Hampton Institute,
a school for blacks in Virginia. Because the
information was contributed by young black

people, it is more credible than much of that
published by white folklorists of the period.

The Hampton students' material provides an
excellent overview of conjure practices in the
South in the latter part of the nineteenth
century, and because it is presented with little
prejudice, extensive excerpts are given here.
Among the practices of evil conjure reported by
the Hampton students were these:

One instance is given of "toad heads, scorpion
heads, hair, nine pins and needles baked in a cake
and given to a child who became deathly sick." By
another of our writers it is said that "some go in the
woods and get lizards and little ground-dogs and
snakes and dry them and powder them all up
together in liquor and give them to drink, or pick a
chance and put in their food so they can eat it." ...
The theory in regard to the poisonous effects of hair
is thus stated by a boy whose own hair had been
baked in bread and given him to eat. The conjure-
doctor told him that if he had eaten it the hair would
cling round his heart strings and would have af-
flicted him so that he would not be able to work and
after a while it would kill him. It required no belief
in the supernatural whatever to make one afraid of
persons whose business it is to devise poisons to
place in the food of their victims, and, if the
evidence of our collection of compositions is to be
trusted, there was on the plantations in the old days
a vast amount of just that sort of thing ...

The form of the charm which comes most near to
the simple poisoning, of which we have already
given examples, is the passing of the spell to the
victim by handing to him some conjured article or

placing it where he can pick it up. In these examples it is contact alone that transmits the evil; the charm or poisoned thing need not be eaten. A sweet potato on a stump in the victim's potato patch has been known to cause pain just as soon as it is touched by the one for whom it is intended ... In another case a small red bag (presumably filled with occult items) is fixed to the sole of the victim's foot ...

But charms seem to be most frequently conveyed by even more indirect means than those thus far enumerated. A baby is conjured by the presence in his crib of something all wrapped up in hair and all kinds of other queer looking things ... conjure balls, snakes, and all kinds of reptiles are often found in the beds of those who have been 'conjured.' In other cases, the fatal bundle or bottle is secreted in some corner of the room in which the victim lives, or is placed in the road over which he oftenest walks ... poison may be put in a bottle and buried in a path (in some cases upside down) ...

If you fail to get near enough to your victim to place the spell in his room or his hand or his bed or his path, you may yet, if you are skillful, succeed in carrying out your fell design by simply burying your charm under his doorstep or in his yard, where he may never see it, or come in contact with it, but where it will work untold evil to him and his. . . . In one case a bottle full of snakes was buried by the doorstep. The first one who came out in the morning stepped over it and fell. . . . In one case, where there was reason to suspect conjuring, a bottle filled with roots, stones, and red-disk powder was found under the doorstep, and in the yard more bottles with beans, nails, and the same powder. . . . Again, a package in the shape of a brick was found, and inside of it 'a tin trunk and a great many articulate creatures.' Another of our writers tells us that 'some of their simplest things are salt, pepper, pins, needles, blackbottles, and all kinds of roots. I have seen one of their roots which they called the "Devil's shoestring." It is a long, wiry-looking root, resembling the smallest roots of a potato-vine.' [Actually another name for the common plantain, it is used to treat stings and bruises.]

With this variety of gruesome and disgusting things did the plantation conjurers essay to work evil among the credulous people by whom they were surrounded . . .

Benefic conjure, as reported by the students at Hampton Institute, also centered around the conjure doctor:

When it is once decided that the sufferers from mysterious symptoms of any kind have been conjured, there remains no hope except through the conjure-doctor. He must be sent for at once, as delay is dangerous and often fatal. There are few settlements of colored people in which the belief in conjuration is prevalent, in which there is not to be found some person distinguished for his skill as a conjure-doctor . . .

The conjure-doctor has five distinct services to render to his patient. He must 1) tell him whether he is conjured or not, 2) he must find out who conjured him, 3) he must search for and find the 'trick' and destroy it, 4) he must cure the patient, 5) he will if the patient wishes turn back the trick upon the one who made it. . . . A case is mentioned of a girl who had been suffering for a long time from a sore foot until at last a conjure doctor was called to her relief. 'As soon as he saw the foot he said that she was conjured and that it was done by an old man who wanted to marry her, and that it was done at church one night. Then he said, "I will try to cure you in the name of the Lord." Then he asked her for a pin and scratched her foot on the side and got some blood and he rubbed some cream on it and said, "God bless her," and he called her name, and the next morning this girl who had been ill for nine months walked out of doors without crutch or cane.' . . .

Another practitioner arrived when sent for with a bottle filled with herbs, roots, and leaves; with these he made a tea which acted as an emetic, and the patient threw up a variety of reptiles . . .

Either after or before the cure of the patient is well under way, the doctor will make an effort to find the 'trick' or 'conjure,' and to identify the miscreant who has caused the trouble. He may be able to tell immediately without visiting the spot, just where the cause of the trouble is buried. An instance is given of an old man who was visited by a woman who lived twelve miles away and was able to tell the patient after one look at her sore foot exactly the spot in her own yard where, if she would dig, she would find a large black bottle, containing a mixture, placed there by one of her neighbors to trick her. She went home, dug and found it was as he said. . . . The conjure-doctors seemed to have an objection to name the enemy who had cast the spell.

In some cases they would simply undertake to describe him; in other cases a more complicated device was resorted to: They would find a bundle of roots under the doorstep or floor. After they had found the roots they would ask for a flatiron. They would take the iron and a piece of brown paper and draw the image of the person who put the roots there . . .

Had conditions for blacks after emancipation been different, both voodoo and hoodoo, particularly in their more malignant forms, might have died out. But emancipation did not bring real freedom, merely a more benign form of serfdom. So the practices continued, and many have survived as a viable aspect of New World black life to the present day, contributing in no small measure over the years to the continuation of black life. In retrospect, their major contribution was not to bolster the courage of rebelling slaves, although they did serve that function. In terms of the slaves' condition or black-white relations, magic never significantly altered the status quo. But it gave the slaves and later the freedmen, who were effectively denied any semblance of collective power, a measure of individual power.

It has served this function even though, from the start, most whites seemed immune to its effects. Melville Herskovits explained this apparent contradiction well:

The tradition that a certain kind of magic is only efficient in the case of a certain type of people is to be met with widely. 'White man's magic isn't black

man's magic,' a succinct statement of this principle,
was heard on a number of occasions in the interior
of Dutch Guiana. For the Negroes realize that,
lacking belief, supernatural powers cannot work
effectively. Where belief is held, however—and the
matter of belief is not the result of individual
volition, but of early training and affiliation—the
power of these forces can operate in all its strength.

And so, their magic ineffective against whites,
blacks used it against each other.

It can be argued that the persistence of such
magical and mystical-magical practices has
been detrimental to black progress in the New
World. If the energies expended in hoodooing
each other and protecting themselves from
being hoodooed by others had been directed
toward a more progressive and mutually beneficial goal, would not blacks have advanced
farther faster? Did not the mutual suspicion
prevalent in the black community prevent pro-
ductive cohesion? The point is well taken but is
probably too idealistic in its inherent concep-
tions of what might have been. Recall that
magic was employed in encouraging many of
the early slave revolts, but most of these were
put down. The status quo being essentially
unassailable, the slaves and later the freedmen
did what most severely oppressed peoples in
history have done; they turned upon each other.
And yet the means by which blacks turned
upon each other can be seen as the healthiest
means, comparatively. Restricted from the
practice of so many other cultural and social
forms, blacks found a kind of sociocultural

release in the practice of magic and the maintenance of supernatural beliefs. Psychic energy
found a channel for activity here. And since the
larger white society either did not know about,
did not understand, or deprecated those practices and beliefs, these forms constituted one of
the only areas of black life in which they could
find privacy. In sum, voodoo, hoodoo, and their
allied phenomena allowed for their own kind of
cohesion, a perverse kind perhaps, but a cohesion nevertheless. And much, much later, the
mythology and folklore built up over centuries
of belief and practice have proved a considerable source of pride for blacks, not only in the
retention of vestiges of the African heritage but
also in the development of a distinct New
World black heritage.

III

Voodoo and Hoodoo Today

In 1969 a 22-year-old woman dashed into the emergency room of a Baltimore hospital and hysterically begged for help. Her twenty-third birthday was only three days away and she was sure she was going to die before it came. The bewildered emergency room staff calmed her down and asked her to tell them why she believed she was going to die. She had been born on a Friday the thirteenth in the area of the Okefenokee Swamp in Georgia, the young woman explained. After her birth it had been discovered that the midwife who had delivered her was a "voodoo" and that she cursed every child born on such a fateful day. The young woman knew of two other girls born on a Friday the thirteenth in the same area whom the same midwife had cursed. The midwife had predicted that one would never live to be sixteen. That girl had died in a car accident when she was fifteen. The midwife had said that the second girl would never see twenty-one. She had been shot and killed in a gun fight in a night club on the eve of her twenty-first birthday. The third girl faced her questioners in the hospital in Baltimore and told them the midwife had said she would never live to be twenty-three.

Though skeptical, the hospital staff admitted the young woman for observation. The next morning a nurse found her dead in bed. Cause of death was listed as unknown.

In July 1973 some very strange objects were reported found in New York City's Central Park. On one occasion it was the carcass of a chicken; on another, it was a pig's head.

Ridgefield, New Jersey, police reported several eerie findings during the six-month period between October 1974 and April 1975. In the fall they found twelve white wax candles, a bag of oranges and tangerines, and several raw eggs dyed yellow in the English Neighborhood Church Cemetery. They shrugged off the incident as a youthful prank and thought nothing more of it—until February. In that month they found in the cemetery a bloody towel and several severed chickens' heads. Then on Good Friday someone reported finding a blood-stained tombstone and the carcass of a mongrel dog. Searching the area later, the police found the dog's head.

In late July 1976 James R. Rosenfield of Manhattan decided to bicycle up to the Inwood section of the island. Walking his bike along the shore of the Spuyten Duyvil creek, he was astonished to find a pile of dead animals, including three chickens, two ducks, several pigeons and fish, and a baby goat. They lay on a bed of chopped apples, oranges and carrots. On a rock about ten feet away were drawings of a stylized bird and a human figure.

What's going on here? Do these reports indicate a resurgence of voodoo practice? Several
theories have been advanced. Ridgefield, New
Jersey, police consulted experts on witchcraft
and the occult, who suggested the findings in
the cemetery were the work of untrained ex-
perimenters. Police in Manhattan's Central
Park precinct thought that the dead animal
remains found there in 1973 might be the work
of Hispanic immigrants, among whom several
cults, including Santeria, flourish. Police in the
precinct serving the Inwood section of Manhattan theorized that the strange findings there
were tied to the nearby colony of Rastafarians.
Nearly one hundred of them had been living in
the area for about a year. The cult, which
originated in Jamaica, holds that the late Em-
peror Haile Selassie of Ethiopia is God, or Jah,
and that the black man must leave "Babylon,"
or the Western World, and return to Africa.
Since the Rastafarians wear their hair in long
"dreadlocks," smoke massive amounts of mari-
juana, and live communally, it was quite natural for the police to make this association, but
Rastafarians are not known to practice animal
sacrifice as part of their religion.

As to the cause of death of the young woman
in Baltimore, doctors have recognized the existence of self-induced shock brought on by
prolonged and intense emotion for a long time.
But there is no proof that the old midwife was
actually a voodoo.

Still, the tales of voodoo practice continue. In
June 1977 a rural Alabama minister was slain,
allegedly by the uncle of the young woman
whose funeral he was conducting. The minister,

Reverend Willie Maxwell, was suspected of doing away with several family members. He was reportedly a practitioner of voodoo.

In November 1977, five teenagers were arrested for breaking into crypts in two Queens, New York, cemeteries and removing skulls to sell for prices ranging up to $500.00 each to cult worshippers.

In November 1977, police found the frail and dehydrated body of six-year-old Daniel Bush in the basement apartment of a house in Indianapolis. An autopsy revealed, according to a hospital spokesman, "the highest concentration of salt in the bloodstream we have ever seen." Daniel's eight-year-old brother and seven-year-old sister were hospitalized for malnutrition, and their mother, Ms. Trula Bush, was arrested. Mrs. Willa Mayes, forty, with whom Ms. Bush and her children were staying, was arrested for allegedly neglecting her three grandchildren, aged eight, seven, and five, who were also hospitalized for malnutrition. All six children, the reports alleged, had been denied solid food and fed a salt solution in what appeared to be a religious ritual of purification (salt has long been regarded as a purifier in conjure lore).

Further investigation revealed that Mrs. Mayes was a practicing spiritualist who said she had been born with a "caul," or "veil" (remnants of the fetal membrane) over her face and claimed to be able to heal the sick, foretell the future, and administer mystic spells. In the basement where Daniel Bush's body was found were two wooden altars containing a variety of religious objects, including colored candles, a seven-branched candelabrum, pictures and

statues of Christ, a number of bottles filled
with powders and liquids, and other items described as "characteristic of various voodoo
rites." Mrs. Mayes reportedly had traveled frequently to nearby cities, including Louisville,
Kentucky, to meet with fellow believers and
other spiritualists. In Louisville, she had met
Ms. Bush, who had taken her children to
Indianapolis and moved in with Mrs. Mayes
about a month before Daniel Bush had died.

According to neighbors in Indianapolis,
chanting could be heard coming from Mrs.
Mayes' apartment at night. A male neighbor
said, "She told me that at will she could cast a
spell . . . put a whammy on anybody." A female
neighbor said she had had "spiritual visits"
with Mrs. Mayes: "She said she could fix
people, and she could, too. I remember one time
she said somebody had something on me and
we took care of it." The woman refused to
elaborate on how the offender had been taken
care of. A Louisville man named Frank Pollack
reported that the year before Mrs. Mayes had
offered to cure his mother of cancer. He and his
mother had refused Mrs. Mayes' help, and
when Mrs. Pollack died about six weeks later,
Mrs. Mayes had told him his mother's death
was due to her failure to follow directions. She
then told Pollack to burn a book of poems he
had that she said was evil. To get rid of her, he
told her he had burned the book. Pollack was
the only person interviewed who agreed to be
quoted by name. Some did not wish to become
involved in the legal proceedings, but some
feared "hexes" or curses.

The arraignment of Ms. Bush and Mrs. Mayes

was cut short when Mrs. Mayes suddenly fell to her knees with arms outstretched, creating a furor in the courtroom. Ms. Bush informed the astonished onlookers that the episode was a "spiritual reply."

Even the most skeptical watchers of occult practice in the United States admit that witchcraft and black magic are enjoying a minor renaissance here. There is also increased interest in astrology, tarot card reading and palmistry. Police in New York report that fortune tellers and seers have increased by 30 percent in the past five years. Books on occult and spiritualist subjects abound and the proliferating spiritualist supply houses are doing a booming business.

In part, this renaissance is attributed to the sense of alienation and separation, the loss of "mental tranquility," as Joseph Washington, a religious scholar, puts it, that seems to afflict modern Western society. And in part, it is attributed to the general feeling of nostalgia for the past, which is probably also an outgrowth of the current alienation. A renewed sense of history among Americans has led to a plethora of new museums, historic houses, and the like, and if Charles M. Gandolfo had not opened his Voodoo Museum in New Orleans, someone else probably would have.

The Voodoo Museum is not a large enterprise, but it is an active and increasingly popular one. On display are talismans, drawings, masks, drums, and other voodoo artifacts, mannequins dressed to represent voodoo deities, ritual altars, even a small black coffin. The adjoining Gift Shop offers various dolls,

seals, potions, powders, and other voodoo paraphernalia. Gandolfo also organizes historically
accurate reenactments of voodoo ceremonies,
walking tours to traditional voodoo sites (including Calvary Spiritual Church, one of five
voodoo churches in the city, Congo Square,
where voodoos danced on Sunday afternoons,
St. Tammany Parish, where voodoo ceremonies
are said to be held even today, and Bayou St.
John, where voodoos worshipped in the past).
He hopes someday to construct a complete
"Voodoo Village."

Nearly every New Orleans tourist map or
booklet includes the Voodoo Museum and its
walking tours, but despite this evidence of
success as a tourist attraction, the Museum is
not meant to be a tourist trap. Gandolfo is a
real history buff and a man who has a deep
respect for the voodoo tradition, from its beliefs
to its rituals. "As in all belief, the power of
suggestion is the most potent ingredient," he
says. "As in all remedies, the force of positive
thinking is the great healer. And as in all magic,
it is the magical powers of the mind which
accomplish true sorcery."

All of the experts on occult practice, students
of the occult, and the like agree on the psychological bases of the resurgence of occult practice. Where they often differ is in their opinion
of the historical and geographical origins of the
current practices that have been traditionally
identified with black culture. (No one is saying
that the many fortune tellers in New York, for
example, are not primarily gypsies practicing
ancient, European-based, arts).

Some argue that the modern mystical-magical practices generally referred to as voodoo and hoodoo today bear little resemblance to the African traditions. Indeed, they scorn the idea of directly traceable roots and point out that many of the beliefs and practices of New World blacks, at least during the past century, can be just as closely if not more closely associated with European mystical-magical practices and beliefs. On the other hand, there are those who fervently support the tenacity of the African traditions and who feel that most modern voodoo and hoodoo practices are in some way directly traceable to the ancestral homeland. Still others accept dual heritage, ascribing more or less influence to each source. This last view is the most sensible.

Man does not exist in a vacuum. He is affected and influenced by a variety of environmental and social factors, and the strength of this influence depends on the extent and nature of those factors. Blacks have been in the New World for centuries and have had at least some contact with Europeans from the beginning. It stands to reason that over the years they were attracted to, and adopted, certain beliefs and practices of the cultures with which they found themselves in contact. However, blacks have historically been subjected to varying degrees of social isolation in the New World. It's a sociological axiom that isolation helps to preserve certain cultural traits, beliefs and practices which, as isolation lessens, abate in force in their native culture while at the same time beginning to influence the surrounding cultures. Give and take between cultures is inevitable. This process does not impair the legitimacy of either culture, but makes them more interesting and probably more viable.

The existence of parallel, independently developed beliefs in different cultures must also be taken into account. Just as a number of world religions share certain basic assumptions and even myths, so do a variety of magical systems. Newbell Puckett conducted considerable research into folk beliefs of southern whites and blacks in the 1920s and 1930s. He pointed out parallels in European and African uses of hair and nail cuttings of the dead for evil purposes, although these goals were more evil in African than in European practice. Other parallels can be found in the beliefs that sleeping in the moonlight will cause insanity and going to bed hungry encourages sin. Still other parallels involve the mystical significance attached to certain numbers, among them 3, 7, and 9, and the operation of the principle of like-to-like. This principle, which appears to operate in every magical system, holds that an object belonging to a person can be used to represent that person, or that the properties of natural objects can be used for unnatural purposes, for instance running water to "run" someone away.

There are other probable parallels between European and African beliefs and practices. One is the belief that a magical item used in conjure must not be seen, and certainly must not be touched, by anyone else lest it lose its power. Another is the practice of ascribing particular colors to certain powers and magical objects. In the West African mystical-magical systems, various colors were believed to be favored by particular gods. Red was one of those, and may explain the predominance of red flannel bags to contain hoodoo "hands," or bags of roots or powders. Different colored candles are also used in specific hoodoo rites. Perhaps this is a general human tendency applicable to all magical belief systems. Time of day, too, often plays a role in the performance of voodoo and hoodoo, as it does in European magical practice.

Candle burning for magical purposes as well as other practices of, for example, most palmists and readers, are of European origin as are a variety of superstitions held by New World blacks. Also, any beliefs or practices with directly traceable Biblical origins must be accorded European influence. But a number of beliefs and practices can be traced with some certainty to West Africa, and these are of primary interest here.

One of the most basic and important is the syncretism between good and evil that existed in West African belief and that has survived almost intact among New World blacks. This belief, perhaps more than any other, can be ascribed to African and not to European influence, for in the European tradition there has always been a distinct dichotomy between good and evil. The popularization of psychological principles has made this idea far more acceptable to those of European heritage today than it was to their forebears. To them, accustomed to seeing things in terms of either/or, good/bad, black/white, the African belief seemed at best naive and at worst downright immoral. To us, who have learned from psychology that supposedly antisocial behavior can be healthy, that love can be a form of tyranny, and that a lack of structure can be restrictive, the African belief that good and evil are but two sides of the same coin is seen as realistic; and a world view that emphasizes relativity, not absolutes is recognized as far healthier than an opposite world view.

That attitude enabled members of conquered African tribes to adopt the gods of 'their conquerors, and vice versa, allowed Africans enslaved and brought to the New World to adapt to the religions of their masters, when those masters and the nature of those religions permitted. Accepting the one did not necessarily mean rejecting the other.

This syncretism extended to the very charms used in African magical practice, most of which could do good or evil depending on the circumstances of their use. A charm worn or employed by one who wished to protect himself would not only ward off evil but could also cause evil to befall those who would do harm to the wearer or user. A charm planted to hurt another, if discovered by the intended victim, could be used to hurt the person who planted it in the first place. Among North American blacks this latter practice came to be known as "turning the trick."

One of the most identifiable traits of black conjure in the New World has been syncretism of elements and items. In the chapters containing conjure "recipes" the same elements are encountered over and over again—eggs; graveyard dust; crossroads or forks in the road; the numbers three, seven, and nine; pins and nails;

red flannel bags; yellow homespun; urine; feces and menstrual blood; shoes and other items of clothing; black cats and black hens; doorsteps and the interior and exterior corners of houses—employed alternately for good or evil, depending on circumstances. Though prayer is encountered more frequently in benefic conjure, it is nevertheless present in malefic conjure as well.

Other, specifically African elements may be identified with some assurance. The power attributed to running water is one. As will be seen in the following chapters, it occurs again and again in practices involving insanity and forced departure. The power of lightning and wood struck by lightning is another, as is the power of the crossroads. Puckett reported that among some black southerners a person wishing to become a practitioner of black magic had to go to a crossroads and pray to the Devil for nine days and nine nights. The practice of keeping a frizzled, or curly-feathered, hen in one's yard to scratch up evil conjure continues in parts of West Africa just as it does in parts of our rural South. In the late 1890s, Miss Ruby Andrews Moore reported in an article in the *Journal of American Folk-Lore,* "Superstitions of Georgia," a remedy for poison that included the drawing in the sand of a design similar to that used by Yoruba as a decorative and religious motif. Later on you'll see that one is supposed to be able to secure general luck and protection by wearing a silver dime around one's waist. In another chapter a knotted yellow cloth around a woman's waist is believed to ensure her husband's sexual loyalty.

That waist beads were a common adornment in West Africa is probably no mere coincidence. Many more New World black beliefs and practices can be traced to West Africa; this isn't an exhaustive list. Nor should we ascribe to today's conjurers any direct knowledge of the West African roots of much of their practice. As Melville J. Herskovits aptly put it: " . . . minutiae can persist after the broader lines of ritual procedure and their underlying rationalizations have been lost."

Over the years the distinctions between voodoo and hoodoo have been blurred until they are commonly used interchangeably. Of the two, voodoo seems most in need of legitimization in our modern culture. Many people in New Orleans, for example, want to get away from the images of serpent rites and dolls stuck with pins. The term spiritualism is favored in some parts of the region. "I am a spiritualist," said Mother W., who was born in the bayou country near Algiers and who now practices in New Orleans. "I help people who come to me with their problems. I pray and use my powers to help them find the way." Hoodoo is a still more generalized term than voodoo and can be applied not only to complex, magical practices but also to simple medicinal procedures and even to superstitions. When a distinction is made, however, hoodoo is retained to describe the more complex procedures, while the simple practices and superstitions are categorized as signs. Though the distinction is not clear-cut, the following examples may serve to illustrate the difference:

Placing a charm or hiding an object in one's

yard or the yard of one's neighbor is hoodoo. The belief that dropping a knife portends a male visitor is a sign. Wrapping a knife in cloth of a certain color and doing prescribed things with that knife to achieve a goal is hoodoo. Mother W. related an incident that serves as an excellent example of the operation of signs: "When I was a girl I remember a bird got into my grandmother's house. A bird in the house means somebody in your close [immediate] family is going to die before the week is out. It was a blackbird and my mama knew it meant grandmama was going to die. I remember how they tried to kill that bird, but it was too late. My grandmama and my mama cried and prayed the whole week. When I came by my grandmama's house Saturday morning, she didn't answer. I ran to get my mama, but grandmama was dead."

Sometimes further distinction between hoodoo and signs involves the respective practitioners. The average individual is usually capable of the simple practices and beliefs that are signs. Successful hoodoo practice depends on one who by heritage, training or supernatural selection knows its secrets.

Modern practitioners are not easily identifiable. In the past they were more inclined to dress differently from others, to wear amulets, to have pet cats, or to keep live fowl. Nowadays they are best identified as the people in a community who have more than the average number of visitors per day or per week. They tend to be older—in their 50s or 60s, although there are a few younger persons who are learning the practice. Frank Hendricks, proprietor of the Dixie Drug Store in New Orleans, testifies, "We get all ages. There is a preponderance of people in their 50s, but younger people continue to come into the field." In most cases initiates are trained by apprenticing to veterans, or by learning from their parents, as is the case with Mother W., who recalled: "People used to come to my mama when they had problems and she would help them. She wouldn't let me watch her work when I was real young, but I remember when I was almost grown she started teaching me the secrets."

Exceptions to this customary method of initiation include those who by circumstances of birth are automatically possessed of occult power. Someone born with a "veil" over his face is believed to be a special person who can summon spirits and communicate with the dead. "They are chosen," said a neighbor of Mrs. Mayes, the woman arrested in Indianopolis. If the person is the seventh daughter of a seventh sister, she has extra special powers. And one nonpractitioner in Mississippi told me in some detail about a "Hoodoo School" in New Orleans to which Miss E. of Sebastopol had gone. This is how Miss E. had described the experience to her:

They say you have to go through seven devils. They got big rooms like the hospital. You have to go through seven rooms before you can be [a hoodoo practitioner] because you have to have nerve. There are different kinds of things you see, and you can't go through all them changes at once.

The first room has snakes and different animals be trying to eat you up and crawl all over you. The second one is blood and you have to walk through blood and stuff. The third room is where you drink the blood. If you are able to drink the blood in the third room, why you automatically go through the whole thing. [In other words, the first three will either make or break you.] In the seventh room, that where you pass your test, like passing into the next grade at school. But if you don't make it through that third room, you have to do it all over again, because it takes people with nerve to do stuff like that.

The above should probably be viewed with some skepticism, although the informant firmly believed Miss E.'s story about this "Hoodoo School" in New Orleans. It is possible that Miss E., whom I interviewed and who told me no such story, was merely exercising her knowledge of human nature. Clearly, anyone with a reputation for being strong enough to go through those seven rooms must have some powerful potions to dispense. One very identifiable trait of successful practitioners is a good, practical sense of psychology not to mention more than the average amount of extrasensory perception and skill in character analysis.

Practitioners are, and always have been, professionals. They charge for their services; the fee scale depends on the area in which they work and on the spell or cure they are asked to perform. Mother W. charges only token fees, but she is an exception. In a small town in Alabama in the 1940s and 1950s fees were generally $3, $5, and $7. Nowadays they are more likely $10, $15, and $20. In larger towns and cities $25, $75, and $100 fees are not uncommon, and cash is preferred. In smaller towns payment is sometimes made in produce, and some practitioners will accept food stamps. Some practitioners are nearly illiterate, others quite well educated; some perform more elaborate rites, others very simple ones. Some freely incorporate religious elements in their work, others avoid such elements or, when they do use them, do so sparingly. Most are part-time conjurers, but not necessarily by choice. As one informant in Mississippi put it, "People are not putting spells on people like they used to. Used to be, you'd do at least three spells a day. But the people [who believed] have gone to different cities and there aren't so many older people around."

There are not many practitioner purists around anymore either. Although various sources whose recipes are given in the following pages sometimes specified obtaining roots directly from the woods or graveyard dust directly from the cemetery, there is some doubt that they actually go through all that trouble. Increased urbanization and the declining areas of natural flora and fauna, for example, have limited the sources of many natural elements. And the proliferation of hoodoo supply concerns and mail order houses has rendered the gathering of conjure supplies in the field, as it were, almost unnecessary. Just about every root and herb, oil and potion, is available commercially, and nowadays most natural items used in conjure "grow" not in the worker's garden or environment but in the hoodoo supply store. As

an illustration, here is a *verbatim* list of herbs
stocked by just one such outlet, Mi-World
Bookstore in Hialeah, Florida:

§§ Adam and Eve
Angelica
Anise seed
Arrow root
Asafaetida
Ash leaves
Anise stars
Aloe
Allspice
Alfalfa
Althea
Ague
Boneset
Broom tops
Bayberry
Bay Laurel leaves
Beth root
Betony
Black snake root
Blessed Thistle
Blue Vervain
Blood root
Buchu
Burdock
Bladderwrack
Cedar Bark
Cinquefoil

Cowslip flowers
Cayenne pepper
Celandine
Catnip
Chamomile
Cinnamon
Clevers
Coltsfoot
Comfrey
Coriander seeds
Celery
Couch grass
Cubeb Berries
Damiana leaves
Dandelion
Devils shoestring
Dragons blood
Devil's bit
Devil's cup
Devil's club
Dog grass
Dulce
Ditany of Crete
Elecampane
Eucalyptus
European Golden
Rod

Fennel seed
Five fingers grass
Elder flowers
Flax seed
Fo ti tieng
Figwort
Fleabane
Foenngreek seek
Galangal
Ginseng
Golden Seal
Gotu kola
Guinea red pepper
Gavel root
Hemlock
Houseleek
Hearts Ease
Holly
Holy
Heal All
Hops
Hawthorne berries
Horehound
Hyssop
Irish sea moss
Iron weed
Jalop
John the Conqueror
high and low
Jopo holy root
Juniper berries

Job's tears
Joe Pic
Knot grass
Khus Khus
Kelp
Kava Kava
Kola nuts
Lavender
Lemon verbena
Lobelia
Linden
Lovage root
Lucky hand
Ladies thumb
Lungwort
Lotus
Life everlasting
Licorice powder
Mandrake
Mace
Master of the wood
Mugwort
Mint
Mistletoe
Mullen
Muria Puma
Mustard seed,
black or yellow
Myrrh
Myrtle
Monkshood

Marjoram
Mormon tea
Maiden hair fern
Nettle
Nutmeg (whole or
     powdered)
Orange flower
Poppy flowers, red
Princess pine
Pine
Psyllium seeds
Poke root
Pole cat weed
Paradise seed
Passion flower
Patchouli
Perriwinkle
Pennyroyal
Queen Elizabeth root
Red coon root
Red clover blossoms
Red sandalwood
Rose buds
Rose hips
Rosemary
Rue
St. Johnswort
Sandalwood powder
Sandalwood chips
Sarsaparilla
Sassafras

Scullcap
Spearmint
Sea lettuce
Sage
Senna leaves
Silver weed
Shepard's purse
Skunk cabbage
Slippery elm
Solomon's seal root
Star anise
Sweet flag
Sweet bugle
Sumach
Sourwood leaves
Sacred bark
Sumbol
Tarragon
Thyme
Tonka beans
Trillium
Tormentilla root
Trumpet weed
Uva Ursi
Valerian
Violet
Vervain
Vandal root
Worm wood
Witches grass
Woodruff

Wahoo bark	Yaw root
White oak bark	Yarrow
Walnut leaves	Yerba Santa
Wild grape root	Squill root
Wild lettuce	Peppermint
Yellow dock	Indian psychic root
Yohimbe	Squill root

Such commercial outlets are not new; there were hoodoo supply shops as long ago as the 1890s. According to a Georgian contributor to the *Journal of American Folk-Lore* in 1897, " ... in a certain city of this State there is a market in the drug-shop for the forefeet of moles. These are supposed to assist teething, and for that purpose are hung as amulets about the neck of colored children."

Just as in the past, there is a tendency on the part of many operators of spiritual supply businesses to pay lip service to the false belief that a considerable amount of voodoo merchandise, particularly oils and incense, is made by or used by Hindus. Also, as in times past, these enterprises are careful not to make any claims of supernatural powers for the items they sell. Such phrases as "All items offered are sold only as interesting curios," "All products are based on legend and sold as such," "We make no claims that this . . . has any supernatural power and sell only as a curio," and adjectives such as "alleged" occur again and again in their catalogues and on item labels. Even a booklet available at the Dixie Drug Store is formally titled *"King Solomon's Alledged (sic) Guide to Success? Power!"*

And yet the ingredients and recipes they sell appear to work. Frank Hendricks has operated the Dixie Drug Store in New Orleans for thirteen years. "Over the years there have been some astounding successes," he says, "I could count on one hand the complaints of failure." He and his employees prefer to direct customers seeking advice to one of the how-to books and booklets they stock rather than to dispense such advice themselves. One reason, of course, is that they do not want to be blamed if the recipe or procedure they suggest doesn't work. Another reason, as explained by employee Joseph Bush, is that, "Just about every day people ask advice and if you get involved you take too much time with one customer."

But there are times when Bush has relented. "There was one woman who was trying to buy a house and she was wondering what she could use to make the seller come over in her favor—you know, in price and agreeing to sell it to her. I told her to burn a Praise and Hope candle. Write the name of the person who was selling the house and the name of the attorney who was handling it on a piece of parchment paper nine times and her name nine times over it. Set the candle on top of the paper, make her wish and say the twenty third Psalm—the twenty third Psalm is the most successful psalm. You write the names to conquer them, and nine times is spiritual—nine or seven, but mostly nine. It worked for her—she got a four-bedroom house."

Bush has also been known to give advice to customers on how to uncross tricks put on them by neighbors and what to do for luck in gambling. "Then again," he adds, "I tell them that without prayer none of this is going to work." Frank Hendricks agrees: "Faith plays a big part." Over and over again I encountered similar sentiments. Mother W., who is Catholic, is proud that she has never missed a Sunday Mass—"excepting some years back when my back was giving me problems. I go to church three-four times a week to pray. I light my candles. You have to pray to work the magic. God don't help you unless you give him his due. With God's power, I can do his work. Without it, I can't do a thing."

Even if one is not very religious, one has to believe in the efficacy of conjure in order for it to work, either for good or evil, and if the recipes presented in the following chapters seem at times comical, or at least hard to take seriously, you would do well to bear in mind that hoodoo and voodoo are no laughing matter—to those who believe.

In the following chapters, most of the voodoo and hoodoo recipes are presented under two rather arbitrary headings—to do ill and to do good. This dichotomy is in many ways an outright heresy, and at the least, far more European than African or even Afro-American. I concede arbitrariness and have unavoidably imposed my own morality in the organization of these two chapters. The final two chapters of recipes are not organized that way. They comprise conjures relating to love and to law, in both of which areas it would be an extreme disservice to impose arbitrary moral judgements. In love, for example, if a woman uses conjure to keep her husband from going out at night, she can be said to be practicing malign conjure against him. But such conjure is at the same time benign from her standpoint and even perhaps from the standpoint of the relationship. Similarly, with regard to the law, if a man employs some supernatural method to win a court suit, the method can be classified as benign from the viewpoint of the man himself and malign from the standpoint of society. Love and law are thus treated in separate chapters.

For clarity and ease of reading, the recipes are presented in how-to form and addressed directly to the reader. However, you should bear in mind that in many, if not most cases, it is the practitioner, not the client, who engages in these procedures.

19th-century hoodoo dance.
(Drawing by E. W. Kemble. Courtesy of the New York Public Library)

e-enactment of a voodoo ceremony. Because voodoo rites are conducted
secret, practitioners will rarely allow them to be photographed. The
oodoo Museum in New Orleans, however, produces re-enactments based
research and authenticated testimony.
Loas, or supernatural beings, are believed to abide in trees, and trees
emselves are sometimes honored as divinities. Voodoo dances are often
ld around trees in St. Tammany Parish near Lake Ponchartrain.
ourtesy of Charles M. Gondolfo, Owner, Voodoo Museum, New Orleans)

The serpent-god, or *arpe-reposoir*, will not exercise its power or make known its will except through a high priest or priestess. It is they who decide whether the snake approves the admission of a new member of the cult. The presence of whites is based on authenticated fact; in August 1850 several whites were among the nude women arrested for dancing in a voodoo ritual.
(Courtesy of Charles M. Gondolfo, Owner, Voodoo Museum, New Orleans)

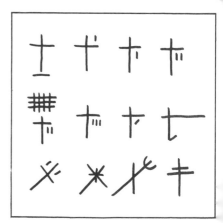

Secret voodoo markings on vaults in St. Louis Cemetery, No. 1.
(Courtesy of Charles M. Gondolfo, Owner, Voodoo Museum, New Orleans)

Luck comes from many sources. Many voodoo believers have made pilgrimages to the tomb of Voodoo Queen Marie Laveau in St. Louis Cemetery, No. 1, in New Orleans. So many pieces have been carved away for charms, so many ablutions administered to it, that it's amazing that the tomb is still intact.   (*Courtesy of Ebony Magazine.*)

Scrubbing steps with urine is believed to be an effective method to keep away evil spirits. (*Courtesy of Ebony Magazine*)

Back in the 1950s, George Bolden, a grave digger in Algiers, Louisiana, claimed to have "the power." Unfortunately, by that time voodoo had become "big business;" one needed the proper equipment to attract customers. Mr. Bolden didn't have the money to invest. (*Courtesy of Ebony Magazine*)

A sampling of voodoo supplies purchased by practitioners and non-practitioners alike. Items shown include incense, floor wash, roots, and a candle. *(Courtesy of Ebony Magazine)*

One type of voodoo doll is made of feathers and wound with black thread. The thread is unwound a little each day, and when the doll falls apart, the victim the doll represents is supposed to die.

(Courtesy of Ebony Magazine)

Representation of the god Exu. The worship of this god in New Orleans illustrates the kind of transformation voodoo has undergone through inter-cultural influence. In Fon mythology, Legba is the interpreter of the gods and intermediary between human beings and the divine pantheon. He is also, as is evident here, a phallic god. In New Orleans and environs his name was generally retained as Legba, sometimes Papa Legba. In Brazil he became Exu. He was brought to New Orleans by immigrants from Brazil and adopted by other voodoo worshipers in New Orleans who accorded him a place in their liberal pantheon. *(Courtesy of Charles M. Gondolfo, Owner, Voodoo Museum, New Orleans)*

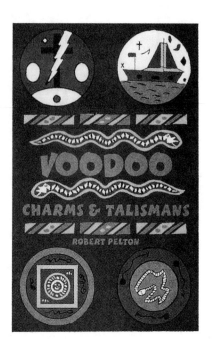

VOODOO
CHARMS & TALISMANS

by Robert Pelton

The power of Voodoo can be yours today!
Absolutely authentic and easy-to-follow instructions to:

· *Make your own talismans*
· *Concoct your own love potions*   **$8.95**
· *Win at games of chance*
· *Summon spirits*
· *Defend yourself against those who may wish you ill*
· *Attack your enemies through devastating spells*

Here are the words, the symbols and the ingredients. Here is all
you need to know to possess power beyond your imagination!

Available from Original Publications or your local bokseller.
See excerpts from this title on the following pages!

TO MAKE YOU
MORE POTENT

This fabulous talisman makes a man or a woman more fertile. It causes pregnancy in couples who are childless and it makes a man's penis more rigid when making love. But this talisman must be taken off and placed under the mattress when having sex in order to be effective.

Embroider in **bright red on white satin** and carry with you. It may also be engraved on a ring or an amulet. *Note:* The crossed penis in the above talisman represents the Voodoo loa *Marinette,* a powerful spirit of fertility and sexuality. The other symbols are simply made to contain and direct her forces as necessary. If thistalisman is used for any other purpose than is outlined above, *Marinette* is said to become very malicious, a constant troublemaker, and an antagonized. She demands an offering of semen rubbed in chicken feathers before unleashing her powerful spirit forces for the good of her subjects. She looks with great favor upon those who have oral sex as a prelude to intercourse. Marinette's special day is Wednesday and a sexual interlude on this day is believed to bring immediate results.

Excerpt from "Voodoo Charms & Talismans"
Chapter 18: To Increase Fertility

TO HELP FIND
A GOOD JOB

This potent talisman brings the possessor good luck when he or she is searching for suitable employment. And it opens many important doors when the need arises. It brings helpful spirit forces to the aid of all people who wish to find a new job. Embroider in **light green silk on silver satin** and carry with you. It may also be engraved on a ring or an amulet.

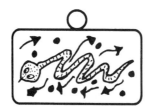

Note: The large headed snake with spots in the above talisman represents the Voodoo loa *Petro Simi,* who can accomplish anything a believer wants done concerning a job. The other symbols are simply made to intensify *Petro Simi's* powerful forces and to help direct them when needed. This spirit requires an offering of white wine and homemade bread before he can be induced to take action in your behalf. Never try to use this talisman for any other purposes than directed above or the wrath of *Petro Simi* may turn upon you.

Excerpt from "Voodoo Charms & Talismans"
Chapter 36: To Get and Hold a Job

TO INCREASE
YOUR SEXUAL CHARM

Pimento Powder	1 teaspoon
Bayberry Incense	1/2 cup
Orchid (crushed)	1/2 cup
Frankincense Powder	1/4 cup
Dill	1/4 cup

Blend all of the above ingredients in a wooden bowl, cover tightly, and set aside in a cool dark place until needed. It is to be burned on *Fast Lighting Charcoal.* Burn a small amount of the mixture just before your loved one is due home, and also burn more while in the throes of passionate lovemaking. Your lover will appreciate you more fully as a result of this, and he or she will cease having sexual relations with others.

This charm is credited to Marie Laveau, a woman who helped thousands of Creole ladies in their *affaires d'amour.* In *New Orleans as it Was,* Castellanos reports: "Her apartments were often thronged with visitors from every class and section, in search of aid from her supposed supernatural powers. Ladies of high social position would frequently pay her high prices for amulets...." Marie Laveau died in 1881, a feeble, quaking old woman with a shriveled, yellowish neck and gray tresses hanging in terrible disarray about her head. Of interest is the fact that when at her zenith as Queen, Marie Leveau never received less than $500 for her unhexing services, and her fee often ran as high as $1000. People waited in line to see her!

Excerpt from "Voodoo Charms & Talismans"
Chapter 31: To Stop a Wandering Lover

TO ATTRACT NEW BUSINESS

This unusual talisman is ideal for making a business more profitable. It was used in early American Voodoo practice by numerous prostitutes in an attempt to attract new customers, and to increase the amount paid for sexual services. Customers coming in once were said to surely return with friends if this talisman were worn during intercourse, or kept under the pillow. Embroider in **gray silk on black satin** and carry with you. It may also be engraved on a ring or amulet.

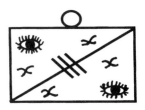

Note: The two eyes in the above talisman represent the all encompassing vision and power of the Voodoo loa *Ezili-Mapyang,* protector of prostitutes and other business enterprises. The other symbols are simply made to intensify the power off this spirit force. *Ezili-Mapyang* always requires an offering of 7 copper pennies placed in a circle around a pink candle. Without this offering she will refuse to take any action on your behalf.

Excerpt from "Voodoo Charms & Talismans"
Chapter 30: To Increase Business

TO AROUSE DESIRE
IN THE OPPOSITE SEX

This fabulous talisman incites sexual feelings in others whenever you happen to come near. It helps the wearer to better understand a prospective lovemaking partner and reveals important clues to assist in a conquest. Embroider in *silver silk on light blue satin* and carry with you. It may also be engraved on a ring or an amulet. *Note:* The bent stemmed flower represents the Voodoo loa *Ezili,* goddess of voluptuousness and femininity. She makes the wearer exude sexuality and magnetism. *Ezili* not only causes arousal in the person who wears this talisman. She also creates unexpected sexual urges in anyone of the opposite sex you come into contact with. This goddess is known as a specialist in oral sex and she induces others to partake in this form of lovemaking. To make a female lover perform fellatio, or a male lover perform cunnilingus, simply whisper the words *Patchouly, Mooga, Karenga, Desular,* during preliminary petting. *Ezili* requires an offering of menstrual blood and semen, blended well, before she will take any action in your behalf.

Excerpt from "Voodoo Charms & Talismans"
Chapter 28: To Make Yourself Sensual

TO AVERT
PHYSICAL HARM

This unusual talisman helps the wearer to avoid all types of physical harm and serious injury. Anyone who possesses such a talisman will never suffer injuries in the home or on a job. It is espesially potent when taken on trips away from familiar surroundings. Embroider in **yellow silk on green satin** and carry it with you. It may also be engraved on a ring or an amulet. ***Note:*** the circle with a dot in the center of the triangle represents the Voodoo loa *Gran Siligbo* who is a friendly and protective spirit force. He offers his services to anyone who believes in him and who will wear or carry one of these special talismans. The other symbols are simply made to keep his power close to the talisman's possessor. *Grim Siligbo* likes a simple offering of a spool of black thread before he will take any action in your behalf. Seldom will this loa ever fail the person who truly has faith in him.

Excerpt from "Voodoo Charms & Talismans"
Chapter 14: To Avoid Injuries

IV

To Do Ill

Folklorists and students of the occult frequently refer to evil occult and magical practices as *maleficia*. Southern Negro terms for malign practices include curse, trick, conjure, root, fix, voodoo and hoodoo. All can refer to ill-doing of some sort, but in another context several of these terms can also be used to identify benign practices.

It is extremely difficult nowadays to find a practitioner who will admit to engaging in malign conjure, and doubtless it is less commonly practiced now than when conditions of black life in the United States were worse. Frank Hendricks, proprietor of the Dixie Drug Store in New Orleans, estimates that only about two per cent of the workers with whom he has come in contact over the last thirteen years have practiced unabashedly evil conjure, although he admits the percentage is higher in cases such as inducing a neighbor to move, or creating confusion in a neighbor's home. One of Hendricks' employees, Joseph Bush, more readily admitted to knowing of practitioners of evil conjure and even mentioned a woman called

Onita who, he said, had dropped out of sight a few months before the interview. Some of my other sources were more generous in their estimate of the number of malefic conjurers practicing now. Malefic conjure is certainly not at all a lost art. Conditions for black Americans have not been improved very long, and in some areas have not improved measurably at all.

Studies of malignant magical practices in Africa suggest a relationship between them and mortality and morbidity rates. In *The Forest of Symbols* Victor Turner reports, "Analysis of witchcraft ought in future to include local statistics of disease and death. For surely it is the sudden and unpredictable onset of severe illness which partly accounts for the random and motivelessly malignant character ascribed to many aspects and types of witchcraft? ... A major feature of witch beliefs ... is that they are attempts to explain the inexplicable and control the uncontrollable by societies with only limited technological capacity to cope with a hostile environment. . . . Constant exposure to ugly illness and sudden death, and the need to adapt to them swiftly, have surely contributed to the formation of these ugly and irrational beliefs. Once formed, the beliefs feed back into the social process, generating tensions as often as 'reflecting' them."

The environment in West Africa during the slavery period was, and remains in many sections today, hostile to human life. Without the technology to combat disease, mortality and morbidity rates are still high, and witchcraft and sorcery are still blamed. Killing by means of dolls or figurines, by the introduction into the victim's body of poisonous or supposedly poisonous substances, by the burying of charms in a path frequently traveled by the intended victim, and by many other devices are all acknowledged examples of evil conjure in parts of Africa today. Similarly in the United States, where black mortality and morbidity rates were, and continue to be, among the highest in the population, it is easy to see how these practices have persisted. The Supreme Court Brown vs Board of Education decision and the legislative gains engendered by the Civil Rights Movement are barely two decades old. The New South is younger than that. All of my sources, practitioners and nonpractitioners alike, were familiar with a variety of malefic conjure, most of which is presented in the following pages. And as you'll see in the chapter on beneficia, if there were not a considerable amount of malefic conjure still being practiced there'd be no need for the plethora of potions and procedures aimed at combatting it.

§§§   To Kill Someone

According to my sources, not much killing is done anymore. One reason given by several of them is that it is just too expensive—up to $500 in good times, although when times are hard workers tend to lower their fees in order to stay in business. Another reason is that the law does not look favorably on murder, even, nowadays, that of one black by another. No practitioner I met would claim any direct experience with death conjure, but all knew of at least one fellow worker who was not averse to performing such conjure under special circumstances, and most were familiar with one or two methods to bring about death through conjure.

The principle of like-to-like is highly operative in death conjures, which are sometimes called "killing hurts," and perhaps the first object that comes to the layman's mind when death conjure is mentioned is the so-called voodoo doll, a symbolic representation of the victim. Zora Neale Hurston encountered an extremely elaborate rite in New Orleans, which she recounted in the *Journal of American Folk-Lore* in 1931. The portion of that rite involving a doll follows:

§§ **Make a coffin one-half foot long. Dress a small doll in black and put the doll in the coffin. Write the victim's name on paper and put it in the coffin under the doll. Don't cover the coffin. Dig a trench much longer than the coffin. Take a black cat and put it in the grave. Cover the open grave with cheese-cloth and fix it so the cat can't get out. Take [a] black chicken and feed it one-half glass of whiskey in which a piece of paper with the victim's name has been soaked. Put the chicken in with the cat and leave them there for a month. They will die. Then put the coffin in and bury it with a white bouquet at the head and foot.**

Only one of my practitioner-informants mentioned dolls, in the following procedure to keep a person frustrated and unsuccessful:

§§ **Write the name of the victim on parchment paper. Make a slit in the back of a doll made of black cloth and put the paper in it. Put cayenne pepper in the slit with the paper and sew up the doll with black thread. Tie the doll's hands at the back and place it in a kneeling position in a corner that is untrafficked. As long as the doll is undisturbed, the person represented will be "kept down." You may subject it to other indignities—kick it, blindfold it. Corresponding problems will befall the victim.**

Although most of the practitioners interviewed said the use of dolls has declined, a variety of dolls are available at many spiritualist supply sources. The Dixie Drug Store does not stock them, but according to Frank Hendricks the store receives several inquiries every year about dolls. He also knows of people who make their own dolls. Mi-World Bookstore in Hialeah, Florida, does stock voodoo dolls, among them a black one for "curses, hate, evil." Handmade of cloth, it is about six inches tall and comes packaged with a name tag, pin, card, and instructions for $5.00. Mi-World also carries a "Haitian Dressed Coffin" for $7.00.

The 7-African Powers Curio Shop in Houston, Texas, offers the best voodoo doll service that I have come across. They stock black, red, and green dolls, undressed $3.00, dressed $6.00. "Send persons Name, piece of their HAIR and CLOTH from clothing or picture." "You need one doll for each person. Spell works faster with personal items belonging to the person representing the doll attached to the doll. In casting spell stick with a pin while talking to it."

The Gift Shop at the Voodoo Museum in New Orleans stocks a variety of voodoo dolls. These include:

§§ **Voodoo Witch Doll (with apple face)** **$6.50**
Voodoo Mini Moss Doll (8" tall stuffed with moss from Louisiana swamps) **2.50**
Voodoo Moss Doll (sack cloth stuffed with Spanish moss) **3.25**
Moss Doll (authentic voodoo doll; large; stuffed with moss) **3.50**
Original Hexing Doll (blue denim and moss) **3.50**
Rope Voodoo Doll (made of rope and cloth) **2.95**
Haitian Voodoo Doll **1.50**

Once photography was perfected and photographs became generally available, they frequently replaced dolls in both malign and benign conjure. Following are some "killing hurts," utilizing photographs provided by Mrs. S. of Charleston, S.C., and Dr. T. in New Orleans:

§§ **Take a photograph of the intended victim and place its face against the north side of a tree. Drive a nail into the photograph. For the next nine mornings drive nine more nails (one each morning) into the photograph. The victim will become progressively weaker and die on the ninth day.**

§§   Take a photograph of the intended victim and put it up on your wall. Shoot at it with an unloaded gun, cursing the person as you pull the trigger. Do this for three mornings and think evil thoughts of the person for the rest of the day. By the fourth day, he will be dead.

§§   Make (or purchase) a small coffin and dress it with the blood of a black chicken or a black cat. Take a photograph of the intended victim and stick twelve pins into it, the twelfth pin right into the heart area. Curse the victim as you are sticking the pins in. Place the photograph inside the coffin and bury it. The person will either die from a hemorrhage or from suffocation.

§§   Obtain a lock of the intended victim's hair as well as his or her photograph. Bury the two together, preferably in mud or in a moist area where the objects will disintegrate quickly. As they disintegrate, the victim will disintegrate, too—visibly and in like manner.

Other methods involve an object that belongs to the intended victim—items of clothing, urine and excrement, hair, and the like.

§§   Obtain a piece of the intended victim's hair and place it in a small, specially prepared (or purchased) coffin. Take the coffin to the graveyard and bury it. The person will die in three days.

§§ Obtain a lock of the intended victim's hair and place it in an egg shell. Throw the egg into a stream and curse the person. As the egg floats downstream the victim's health fails and he eventually dies.

§§ Get some of the intended victim's urine, put it in a bottle and add graveyard dust [available at many spiritual supply stores as well as in the field.] Shake it well and stop the bottle tightly. Bury the bottle three feet down in the ground near the person's doorstep or other area over which the person is certain to walk. Once the intended victim has walked over the spot, he will be unable to urinate and he will die—unless another worker locates the bottle and digs it up. The practitioner in Montgomery who told me of this procedure saved a client by finding such a bottle "a number of years ago."

§§ Obtain some of the intended victim's urine and put it in a bottle. Add freshly squeezed lemon juice and red pepper and shake up the bottle. Bury the bottle upside down in the ground and after you have covered the hole with dirt, stomp on the spot and curse the person. The person will die of de-hydration.

§§ Get some of the intended victim's excrement when it is fresh. Place it in a jar and add some graveyard dust. Bury the jar, cursing the individual as you do so. He will be unable to have a bowel movement and will die nine days later.

§§ Obtain some of the person's excrement and take it to an old, rotting log (or tree, depending on the source—one informant specified green wood). Bore a hole in the log and put the excrement in it. Plug up the hole with a piece of wood. Depending on the informant, you then either leave it alone, or you return regularly to the tree or log and pound the wooden plug. The victim will have his bowels "locked" and will die.

§§ Get a sock or stocking belonging to the intended victim. Put graveyard dirt in it and bury it under the victim's front steps. In three weeks the victim will be dead, having mysteriously withered away.

Dr. T. in New Orleans spoke of workers who kill by means of candles, or "burning candles on" someone. According to him black candles cause a slow death, and red candles a quick accidental death. The actual candle burning is accomplished by various rites, the nature of which depends on the practitioner.

§§§ To Cause Live Creatures in the Body

The malefic practice that caused me to shudder most violently as a child involved the introduction of creatures such as snakes and spiders into a victim's body. This is usually effected with normal-looking food, which is why I was cautioned about eating in other folks' houses. One suffering from such a condition eventually dies, but it usually takes a long time:

§§ Extract the blood from a snake by puncturing an artery and allowing the blood to drip into a container. Feed the liquid blood to the intended victim in food or drink and snakes will grow inside him.

§§ Kill a snake cruelly and make sure he is still alive when you extract the blood from him. Let the blood dry and feed it to the victim in food or drink. Eighteen days later, small snakes will be present in the victim's veins.

§§ Get earthworms and put them inside a fish. Fry the fish and serve it to the intended victim. In three days the victim's intestines will be rife with worms.

§§ Obtain two creatures, usually spiders or snails; kill one and put both in a jar or other container. Put the container somewhere undisturbed. Eventually the live animal will eat the dead animal. Then, kill the live animal and dry it over a flame. Powder it up and feed it to the intended victim. In nine days live creatures will infest the body.

§§ Take a scorpion or a poisonous spider. Impale it on a long needle and let it dry. Pound it up into a powder and sprinkle that powder on the intended victim's food. In time live scorpions will grow in the body, and not only will they cause discomfort by

their very presence, but also they will secrete their
poisonous venom into the veins.

§§§   To Make Someone Ill

There are a variety of ways to cause illness that
are not necessarily fatal. Such tricks cost less
than "killing hurts" and are less risky for
practitioner and client. They run the gamut of
bodily areas affected, from head to foot. To
begin with, here are some methods for causing
general illness:

§§   Take some bark and some root from a persim-
mon tree and some of the root of a fig tree. Boil these
three ingredients in water. Then add some graveyard dust and dissolve it well. Go to the home of the
intended victim with the liquid in a small vial. Drop
one drop just inside his door and another three
drops inside his home. The person will become
mysteriously ill.

§§   Obtain a piece of the intended victim's hair and
a piece of his clothing. Write the person's name and
age on a piece of parchment and put all three items
in a bag with some graveyard dust. Bury the bag
under the person's doorstep. The victim will lose all
his energy and never regain it as long as the bag is
undisturbed.

§§   Write the victim's name on a piece of parchment nine times with indelible ink. Catch a fish, make a small slit in the stomach and insert the paper. Then sew up the slit and toss the fish back into the water. As long as it floats in the water, the person will feel weak and ill.

§§ Obtain a soiled piece of the victim's clothing. Put it in a jug or large jar full of water and stop it loosely so that when it is upended the water will seep out. Bury it upside down in the ground. As long as the moisture seeps through the cloth, the victim will stay sick, and if all the moisture seeps out of the container it can be dug up and refilled.

And here are recipes aimed at specific parts of the body:

§§ To cause headaches, put some graveyard dust in a small bag and hide it in the person's pillow.

§§ To cause a sore foot, take snake blood and ammonia, mix them together and allow them to dry. Then take a piece of glass, crush it up and mix that with the dried blood and ammonia. Sprinkle the mixture in the victim's shoes and he will develop sores on his feet that will not heal.

§§ To cause someone to have chills, take a long piece of string and tie it full of knots, repeating the intended victim's name as you tie each knot. Bury the knotted string under the person's doorstep. As soon as he walks over it, he will begin to have chills, and they will not abate.

§§   To cause a rash, take the root and bark of a fig tree and boil them. Drop nine black peppercorns into the resulting liquor and boil it down again. Sprinkle it over the person's food and he will break out into a rash from head to foot.

§§   To cause kidney failure, go to the person's home late at night with a large bucket of water. Pour out some of the water three times in front of the house, three times on each side, and three times at the back. Each time you pour, say out loud that you want the person to lose control of his kidneys. Thereafter, every time you pour a full bucket of water on the ground, the person will lose all control, which can be highly embarrassing.

§§§   Birth and Labor Maleficia

The previously quoted excerpts from the Hampton students' compositions included conjures aimed at children and babies. I found more, and there are even a few evil conjures aimed at causing a woman to have a hard labor or to miscarry. According to Miss E. in Mississippi, there used to be considerably more; and it is very likely that there is a direct correlation between the decline of infant mortality rates among blacks, and the attendant decline of such practices, there having been progressively less need in this century to explain the traditionally high rate of miscarriages among black women.

§§ Obtain a piece of the woman's underclothing, preferably a slip. Tie nine knots in it, cursing the woman with each knot. By this time the slip should measure approximately the length of a baby. Then knot it three more times. Bury the knotted slip under the woman's doorstep, and soon after she walks over it nine times she will miscarry. The knots symbolically tie up the fetus.

§§ To cause hard labor, obtain the woman's underpants and pull them apart at the seat. Then bury the torn panties under the house or doorstep and the woman will have a breach birth.

§§ If a woman suspects another woman of carrying her own husband's child, she can make the birth very long and difficult. Take a snail from its shell and iron the snail into the husband's underwear. The birth will proceed at a "snail's pace."

§§§ To Cause Insanity

Returning to the article based on the compositions of Hampton Institute students, we find a variety of instances where conjure was blamed for insanity:

. . . many cases are cited where the insane patient is regarded as "conjured" by his relative. One woman could not go further than a mile. "When she had walked a mile she would get out of her head so she would have to stop, so she could gather her mind to go back." A girl when conjured, "ran wild and drowned herself." . . .

It is unnecessary to cite all the instances given in the compositions. They are numerous enough to go far beyond proving that insanity on the plantation was often laid to "conjuration" and consequently took in the patient the form that the belief in conjuration would naturally give it, just as in New Testament times it was believed to be demoniacal possession and took that form in its manifestations.

Some eighty years later there are still many methods and recipes for causing insanity, almost all of which, at least in my research, involve the hair. Being associated with the head, hair is a natural ingredient for this kind of conjure. Hair was used to cause headaches, and it is an old Southern black belief that when you comb or brush your hair you must be very careful to dispose of any loose strands, lest the birds get it and build a nest with it and cause you headaches. Hair employed in insanity conjure is usually either hidden in a tree or tossed into running water.

§§ Hair is placed in a tree much the same way as is excrement in conjures aimed at "locking" the bowels. Depending on the informant, the tree can be a hackberry, a young tree, or any tree at all. After obtaining some of the victim's hair, bore a hole in the tree and place the hair in it. Then plug up the hole. Some informants specified using the same wood that came out of the hole, others any piece of wood. In a matter of days, the person will be nervous, given to hallucinations, quite crazy.

The specification of hackberry by a source in Kentucky is interesting and quite appropriate here, because the hackberry tree is particularly susceptible to a disease called witch's broom, caused by a mite and a fungus. Hackberry trees so blighted can be found in Central Park in New York City. Actually the effect is quite attractive, particularly in winter, and interestingly when the hackberry is in foliage the witch's broom can easily be mistaken for a bird's nest.

§§ Wrap a piece of the victim's hair in tinfoil and throw it into a stream of running water.

§§ Take three strands of the person's hair and bind them up with black silk thread. Carry the hair in your pocket for three days, then toss it into a stream of running water.

Other examples of the use of hair to bring about insanity:

§§ Obtain a piece of the intended victim's hair and singe it lightly over an open flame. Then bury it deep in the ground to cause him to lose his mind.

§§ Take three strands of the person's hair to a place where a road forks. Lay one strand so it points one way, lay one strand pointing the other way, and one strand pointing to the place where the road forks. This symbolically causes the person to be so mixed up he will lose his mind.

§§§ To Cause Disturbance or Confusion

"Some neighbor is always throwing something in front of their doorway or their walkway," said Joseph Bush, speaking of the Dixie Drug Store customers. "That keeps confusion inside their homes." Conjures to cause confusion and home disturbances also remain among the most frequently employed malefic practices. Following are some of the methods I encountered:

§§ Take Crossing Incense and mix it with cayenne and sulphur. Put it in a brand new handkerchief or other piece of new cloth and sprinkle it in the target house. As soon as the house is next swept, the powder will begin to act.

§§ Take graveyard dirt, salt, and Devil Powder and mix them together. Sprinkle that mixture around the interior of the person's home.

§§ Get a cat and dog and set them at each other.

When their hair bristles, cut some from each and mix it with sulphur and cayenne. Sprinkle that mixture inside the target house and the people therein will soon be fighting "like cats and dogs."

§§   Take a small piece of wood and notch it as many times as there are people in the house you wish to disturb. If you have access to the house, nail it in an inconspicuous spot behind the headboard of the bed or on the fireplace mantle. Otherwise, nail it to their door.

§§   Write the names of all the persons in the house on a piece of parchment. Write the names across each other. Nail the paper to the underside of their doorstep, and they will begin fighting with one another.

§§   Catch a catfish and remove the three sharp spikes. Dry them over a flame and pulverize them. Mix them with cayenne. Write the name or names of the persons you want disturbed on a piece of paper three times across each other. Put the powder in the paper, fold it up, and put it in the mouth of the catfish. Throw the catfish back into the water.

§§   Obtain the nest of a dirt dauber, break it apart and mix it with graveyard dirt. Put the mixture in a bottle with War Water and shake it up. Smash it on the person's walkway.

And finally, there are any number of roots, bones, and magical powders or combinations thereof that can be put in bags and placed under the intended victim's doorstep.

§§§ To Make Someone Go Away

As a general rule, when one person dislikes or does not want to be bothered with another, he wishes the other person would simply go away, and in voodoo and hoodoo there are more methods whose purpose is to cause someone to leave than there are methods to cause him particular types of harm. Several of the methods I encountered also involve running water, presumably because it has power not only to cause people to lose their minds but also to cause them to lose themselves as well. On the simplest level, of course, running water carries things, and people, away.

§§ In this instance, it would appear that the conjurer can utilize any type of running water and does not rely on a stream or river. It is necessary to go to the place where the enemy gets his water—a pump or hydrant in a rural area or his own sink elsewhere. Draw some of that water and as the sun rises throw the water as far away from you as possible. Then break an egg on the ground. In three days the person will leave town.

§§ Obtain an article or a piece of the person's

clothing and put it in a bottle. On a piece of parchment, write the person's name and the name of a faraway place. Put that in the bottle, too. Sprinkle sulphur, salt, and red pepper in the bottle and let it sit for nine days. Then take it to a stream and toss it in. Nine days later the person will be gone.

§§   Follow the person whom you want to leave and obtain some of the dirt from his left footprint. Place it in a jar or bottle and stop it up as tightly as you can. Take the vessel to a river or stream and with your back to the body of water, throw the vessel into the water.

§§   Follow the person until he walks where he will leave a footprint. Sprinkle magnetic sand (available at most hoodoo drug stores) into that footprint. With a shovel dig up the footprint and place it in a tin can or box. Carry the container to a river or stream, turn your back to the water, and throw the container over your left shoulder into the water.

Interestingly, the container would be too heavy to float. Even though it would sink, the power of the Magnetic Sand, my source assured me, would ensure the person in question would leave town.

"Not long ago great excitement prevailed in a country district in Mississippi, caused by a young woman who had 'picked up tracks.' It broke up families; everybody was afraid. Nobody knew whose track might be picked up next." These lines were written in 1897, but as the previous two methods indicate, footprints continue to play a considerable role in removal conjures. Following are other removal conjures employing footprints:

§§   **Follow the person and take three grains of sand or soil from his footprint. Place them in a small bag and carry them with you for three days in order to acquire power over them. On the night of the third day, take them to the crossroads and toss them in the direction you want the person to go. Three days later he will leave town by that road.**

§§   **Follow the person and with a spade take up one of his footprints. Put the dirt or sand in a bag made of white cloth (in this case the person is causing you trouble and you want peace, signified by white). Three days later follow the person again, throwing grains of sand or dirt from the bag after him, and he will leave.**

Items associated with the feet can also be used, such as socks, shoes, and even toenails. One informant had heard of burying socks or stockings in a cemetery, and another recounted a tale of how a woman got rid of a relative who had overstayed his welcome. She took his toenail clippings, pulverized them, and served them to him in cornbread. He left shortly thereafter. Here are two recipes that make use of shoes:

§§   **Obtain some Move Quick Powder and sprinkle it all over your floor and in the corners of your house. Take your left shoe and turn it upside down** under your bed. (This is another method for getting rid of an undesirable house guest).

§§   Take the shoe of the person you want to get rid of and take it to the middle of a busy byway. Place it on the road and call out his name, saying that you want him to leave.

Eggs are also frequently used in this regard. Several variations of the following method were encountered:

§§   Obtain a rotten egg and write on it nine times. the name of the person you want to send away. Also write where or how far away you want him to go. At midnight, take it to the person's home and throw it against his door.

Variations included a fresh egg rather than a rotten one, throwing the egg over the left shoulder, and breaking the egg on the roof; a similar method was encountered in court cases. In my Alabama home town, the egg was usually rotten, but instead of being broken it was simply thrown into the person's front yard. Maybe that's why the person didn't always leave on cue.

Black candles can be burned to achieve a similar result; animal manure is popular; photographs, graveyard dust, and coffins were mentioned. Here's a potpourri of methods to make someone go away:

§§   Take a black candle and incise the person's

name on it three times, starting from the bottom so that the name "goes away" from you. Dress the candle with water and sugar, or with honey, or with a sweet-smelling oil. Burn the candle for 30 minutes on each of three consecutive mornings.

§§   In New Orleans one is likely to seek the help of St. Michael for evil and to burn a black candle in front of his picture while praying for the departure of a person.

§§   Go to the home of the person in question late at night, ideally at midnight. Plant your left heel firmly in the dirt and spin around on it nine times. Pick up your heelprint and throw it against the door.

§§   Obtain a photograph of the individual and place it in a small coffin specially made or purchased for the occasion. Bury it deep in the ground and the person will go away.

§§   Take graveyard dirt and sprinkle it in all the corners of the person's house. If you cannot gain admittance to the house, throw it on his front walk.

§§   Take dog manure and mix it with cayenne pepper. Put it in a bag or other container. Write the person's name on a piece of paper three times and fold the paper away from you. Put the paper in the bag or container and bury it.

Two methods I encountered come very close to being signs rather than conjuration. Among the signs, or superstitions, traditionally held by southern blacks are 1) If you sweep a person's feet he will leave; 2) If you do not want someone to return, sprinkle salt after him as he leaves. Here are two so-called conjures involving brooms and salt:

§§ **As the person leaves your house, sprinkle a teaspoonful of table salt in his trail. Take your broom and sweep the salt out of the house, calling his name (quietly) and wishing that he not return.**

§§ **Keep your broom by your door. Every time the person leaves, take the broom and stand it up in his trail and let it fall in the same direction as he went.**

The following method for driving someone away, and last example of malefic conjure, is not exactly conjure either, although it was presented as such. It is included here because of its direct, no-nonsense approach to the problem: Go to the person's home for nine mornings and urinate in front of his door.

V

To Do Good

The largest body of spiritualist practices is today, and probably always has been, benign— aimed at protection, luck, peace, good fortune, and happiness. All the practitioners who were willing to talk at all stressed that their work was of the benefic variety, even though they were conversant with a variety of malefic practices. You'll see, too, that many of the recipes classified as benign are aimed at uncrossing tricks and hurts.

§§§   Turning the Trick

There are still some practitioners who are capable of turning a malefic trick back on the tricker, a practice that, as mentioned earlier, can be isolated as distinctly African in origin and devoid of European influence. To turn a trick back is to find the object that is causing the hurt and, by adding something or doing something to it, cause its evil power to be unleashed against the one who caused it to be laid. Misses Herron and Bacon related the following anecdote which illustrates well the concept of "turnin' de trick":

§§ If the person desires, the trick may now be turned against the person who planted it. Ed Murphy did this by laying the trick he had discovered in a piece of paper, sprinkling quicksilver [in this case, mercury, although the same term is often applied to tinfoil] over it, and setting the paper on fire. The trick exploded and made a hole in the ground a foot deep as it burned up—his enemy soon died. "It is said that if any one tricks you and you discover the trick and put that into the fire, you burn your enemy, or if you throw it into the running water you drown him."

An informant explained this method of turning the trick. The trick in question had been laid in order to make someone ill and involved the use of graveyard dust. The method to turn it back also used graveyard dust:

§§ Go to the graveyard and obtain the finest dust you can find. Mix it with a small amount of chimney soot. Take a box of sulphur and mix the graveyard dust and chimney soot in with it. Stick nine pins in the box, head up, and bury the box under the doorstep of the one who has caused the trick. He will suffer the same malady as his intended victim.

The following method is extremely interesting because of the use of lightning-struck wood. In West Africa one of the most widely recognized forms of punishment of humans by the spirits involved lightning, and wood struck by lightning was considered imbued with magical properties:

§§ **Find a white oak that has been struck by lightning and get nine splinters. Follow the person suspected of laying the trick and put one splinter in each of nine of his tracks. Wish, or pray, that if this person does indeed mean to do harm the trick will turn back on him and cause him to die. (A similar method is used against a person to make him go away.)**

§§ **Go to the tricker's house and get some soil, either from under the doorstep or from under the house itself. Take it to the graveyard and pour it onto a grave. Then take up some graveyard dirt and deposit it under the tricker's doorstep. This turns the hurt back on the tricker.**

Another trick-turning procedure whose origins can with some certainty be traced to West Africa involves belief in the power of running water. In West Africa and in parts of the American South today, some believe that spirits are particularly abundant around bodies of water.

§§ **If a trick is found hidden in or around the victim's home, the victim or conjurer can take it to a river or stream and throw it in. The tricker will go crazy.**

Some sources mention this same procedure for uncrossing tricks alone, not for turning them back.

§§§   Uncrossing Tricks

The majority of methods used against tricks
and hurts today merely uncross the trick or
hurt and do not turn its evil power back against
the tricker. Their aim is simply to relieve the
one who has been tricked. As a general rule,
when a client visits a practitioner he or she is
quite aware that a spell is in operation.
However, if there is any doubt here is a formula
for ascertaining whether or not a trick has been
laid:

§§ **The doctor places a dime under the client's
tongue. If the client is under a spell of some sort, the
dime turns black (an interesting parody of the
medical doctor and his thermometer).**

Misses Herron and Bacon cited the same procedure in 1896:

A conjure-doctor summoned to attend a case of
mysterious illness in a family will frequently begin
his examination by putting a small piece of silver
into the mouth or hand of the sufferer. Should the
silver turn black, there is no doubt about the
diagnosis.

Once the presence of a spell has been ascer-
tained, it is the job of the practitioner to remove
it. The easiest spells to remove are those involving objects hidden in or around the client's
home. Hoodoo practitioners know where to
look, but the lay person familiar with the

principles of conjure is often able to find such simple tricks too. Since the principle of like-to-like is so commonly used, the source of the hurt often gives a clue to the placement of the hurting object. Thus headaches may be caused by something hidden in the pillow or under the head of the bed, impotence by something under the sheet or around the bed. Lameness might be caused by an object hidden in the shoe. Of course if a shoe is missing, it is advisable to go to a practitioner. If he or she cannot locate the missing shoe, there are general uncrossing formulas and methods that can be employed.

King Solomon's Alledged Guide to Success? Power!, a popular item at the Dixie Drug Store, prescribes the following general remedy for driving out evil and bad luck. The necessary ingredients cost, at this writing, $14.70:

§§ 2 Jinx Killer incenses and oil
2 Luck in a Hurry incenses and oil
2 Drive Away Evil incenses
2 Fast Success incenses
Make Your Wish sand
2 Fast Luck Money Drawing incenses
Grandma's Lucky Hand oil

Combine Jinx Killer incenses and Drive Away Evil incenses and burn. Combine Fast Success Incenses, Luck in a Hurry incenses, and Fast Luck Money Drawing incenses. Then burn. Throw a handful of Make Your Wish sand in the air and [wish away the evil and bad luck]. Rub Lucky Hand oil on hands regularly.

Prescriptions for uncrossing specific tricks are more numerous than general antidotes because powerful spells require direct and specific response. Here are two used to uncross really evil tricks the intent behind which is death, the "killing hurt." Both utilize graveyard dust, and although graveyard dust is available commercially, some practitioners prefer to obtain their own. A small quantity of the commercial variety is available for 89¢ at the Mi-World Book Store:

§§ Take graveyard dust and mix it with chimney soot and sulphur. Place nine pins in the box with the mixture, pin heads sticking up. Bury it under the doorstep of the one who has caused the killing hurt.

§§ Take the sole of the victim's shoe and burn it to a crisp. Pound it into a powder and mix it with graveyard dirt. Put that in water and cause the victim to drink it. It will drive out any poison in his body.

Among the most imaginative malefic conjures are those designed to put living things such as snakes and frogs in the body. There are quite a number of ways to get these same creatures out:

§§ To get snakes out of a person's body, catch a frog, cut it open, and place it on the person's belly. Hold it there until the snakes come out of the person's mouth. Depending on the number of snakes in the body, up to three or four frogs may be necessary.

§§ Another way to get snakes out utilizes, appropriately, Snakeroot, the common name for Cnicus benedictys, an anti-rheumatic and diuretic. Mix it with three pieces of oak bark and some running briar root and pulverize the mixture. Dissolve it in water or other beverage and cause the sufferer to drink. Within three days the snakes will be discharged from the body.

§§ If a spider has been introduced into a person's body, it can be exorcised with spider weed, a species of Myosotis. Make a potion from spider weed and bathe the person with it. This is a rather strong remedy; it will cause the person's hair to fall out and his flesh will become dry and scaly. But the spider weed will get inside the body and kill the spider.

§§ Another type of potion made from flora is effective against a variety of creatures. Make a potion by boiling running briar root and saving the liquor. Mix it with fresh milk from a black cow and give the patient a dose every three hours.

§§ Effective against snakes and spiders is a drink whose base is the water in which thirteen pennies have been boiled. Let the water boil rapidly and throw an egg into the pot with enough force to cause it to break. Feed the hot liquid to the victim.

§§ Chew on calamus root (also called sweet flag and sweet root, a stomachic) and bathe every

morning for nine mornings with saltpeter ["salt of
the rock," literally; potassium nitrate]. On the ninth
morning the creatures will pass out of the body.
This is especially good for driving out worms.

§§   Pills can be made from the gall of the earth, also
called rattlesnake root, a bitter-tasting root used for
dysentery and as a tonic for snake and insect bites.
When given to the victim, they cause him to expel
the foreign creatures with his excrement. These pills
made from the gall of the earth are particularly
effective against snakes.

§§   Pills can also be made from the shell of a snail,
pulverized and mixed with whiskey. Once again, the
creatures will be passed out of the body.

§§   A simpler method is to give the person a dose of
salt and black pepper mixed in water and to pray
for the exorcism of the creatures.

   Finally, there are the various medicinal practices that address the problem directly by
causing the victim to vomit up what is causing
him to be ill, whether it is live creatures or
poison:

§§   Obtain mussel shells and boil them until they
are soft. Go to the nearest chinaberry tree and get a
piece of its root. Boil that with the mussel shells.
The resultant elixir will be extremely bitter, due to
the chinaberry root, and, when administered in 3

tablespoons every three hours, will cause the patient to vomit every time until all the poison or creatures are out.

§§ Mix salt with the person's urine and make him drink it. Pray as he is drinking that all foreign substances will be expelled from the body. The person will shortly vomit.

Practitioners who are deeply religious often don't appear to need as much paraphernalia or as many ingredients as do those who are less religious. In the case of a trick involving a client's hair, for example, they need not find the actual hair that is being worked on. Instead, they use the principle of like-to-like and utilize other hair from the client's head. A New Orleans informant places nine new strands of hair on an altar with two white candles. While burning the candles she prays to God to rescue the client's hair from the tricker so the trick will be nullified.

If candles are being used malefically, being "burned on" someone, these candles can be caused to go out. One informant suggested that the victim wear his shoes on the opposite feet and his clothing inside out, for the candles will not burn under such circumstances. Another practitioner suggested the following procedure:

§§ Go outside and circle your house eighteen times, nine times around one way and nine times around the other. When you have completed the eighteenth circle you are back at your door. Stand on the steps and blow hard, symbolically blowing the candles out.

Among the most common malefic beliefs are those calculated to create disturbances in the home and to force a move. Here are three methods for uncrossing such tricks:

§§ This uncrossing method assumes the victim knows the identity of the tricker. Take a rotten egg and go to the tricker's home. Facing away from the house, throw the egg back over your left shoulder. Within nine days the spell affecting your home will be lifted.

§§ To draw back someone who has been tricked into leaving, get nine horseshoe nails. With a sharp instrument make as many notches on the nails as the person is old in years. Then drive them into the person's front doorsill. This will recapture the person's mind and overrule whatever trick caused him to leave.

§§ With this method, it is not necessary to find the source of the trouble, either person or thing. Obtain some holy water, some horse radish, and some ammonia and combine the three ingredients. Sprinkle all the corners of the home and wash the steps with the same mixture. Whatever is buried or whatever evil power is being exercised will be rendered ineffective.

West Africans believed that hags and witches often sucked blood, but most frequently engaged in "riding" their victims. Newbell Puckett reported the following techniques southern blacks used fifty years ago to keep these creatures from their homes:

§§ **Salt sprinkled thoroughly about the house and especially in the fireplace, black pepper or a knife about the person, or matches in the hair all bring dire perturbation to the umbrageous visitors.... Ha'nts, like witches, may also be kept away by planting mustard seed under your doorstep, or by keeping a sifter under your head while asleep.**

There are three points of particular interest in this paragraph. One is the use of matches in the hair, which I encountered as a general protective device. The second is the use of mustard seed and a sifter; and here is what Mrs. S. in South Carolina told me to do to get rid of "hag riding":

§§ **Take equal amounts of mustard seed and flax seed and place them in a sifter and place it on one side of your bed. On the other side, place a pan of cold water. Since hags like neither cold water nor mustard and flax seeds, they will trouble you no more. (She was unable to tell me the purpose of the sifter).**

Another initiate maintained that a combination of flax seed and red pepper kept in a box in the house would prevent a hag from leaving the house once she got in.

The third interesting point in the passage from Puckett is the placement of the sifter under the head, for a source in Birmingham suggested sleeping with a pair of scissors under the head.

Other methods of keeping hags away are: 1) to hang a horseshoe up over the door or window; and 2) to put something new such as a shingle, window, or door on your house.

Finally, here are what might be called miscellaneous uncrossing potions and procedures:

§§ To cure spells that are making one ill, put nine nails or tacks in a large container of water and allow them to rust. Make the sufferer drink the rusty water.

§§ The prescription for someone whose bowels have been "locked up" is to undo directly the trick that has been placed. Remember that to lock someone's bowels, it is necessary to obtain some of his excrement and put it in a hole in a tree and stop up the hole with a peg. To undo the trick, it is necessary to find the tree and cut it down.

§§ A prescription for general illness caused by evil conjure requires beef tongue and beef gall (bile). Boil them in water and honey to make a broth and feed the victim nine drops three times a day for nine days.

§§§   To Cure Alcoholism

All of the practicing voodoo people with whom
I met were well versed in a variety of "home
remedies" for illnesses and ailments that they
admit are not directly traceable to conjures or
hurts. Had the West African belief in the
sources of illness survived intact, however, no
illness would be conceived by them as without
a cause in evil. Although these prescriptions
were not strictly germane to voodoo and
hoodoo, I did record some of the many cures
for alcoholism. Though it is a problem among
most races, alcoholism has been a major pa-
thology among blacks for obvious reasons.
With little money for medical treatment and
little access to most self-help groups, blacks
have traditionally turned to their "doctors" or
root workers for help, or, rather, their loved
ones have done so. Here is a sampling of the
prescriptions for curing alcoholism.

The most common employ foreign substances in the alcohol itself; cigarette ash is
introduced most often. The prevailing wisdom
has it that once a person has drunk whiskey
with cigarette ash in it, he will never drink
again.

A variation is to obtain a rotten log and
pound some of it up fine and put it in either the
person's whiskey, his cigar, or his cigarette.
After he imbibes the whiskey or smokes the
cigar or cigarette he will never again take a
drink.

Fish are an important ingredient in many
alcohol cures. Supposedly the gall, or bile, of

the fish, when placed in the whiskey and shaken up, will render the whiskey an antidote to itself. Others specify the blood of the catfish, generally three drops of blood from the head mixed in with the whiskey, but some cognoscenti prefer blood from the tail, specifically from that of a female catfish at "her time of month." Since blood from the head appears to be just as effective it would seem a waste of time to try to identify a female catfish and to further ascertain whether or not she is menstruating (especially since female catfish do not menstruate).

More ominous, but perhaps more appropriate, are the prescriptions involving the graveyard. Both of the following are interesting in that they reveal the tenacity of the original West African belief that spirits of ancestors can influence life in the temporal world:

§§ **Go to the grave of a deceased loved one and move the headstone. This will wake up the spirit. Call out to the spirit to help the drinker reform and to kill his taste for alcohol.**

§§ **Go to the graveyard with two pieces of board and pace off a grave for the alcoholic. Call out to the spirits to make the alcoholic stop drinking and as you do so pound one piece of board into the mock grave at the head and one at the foot. Pound vigorously.**

§§§ Protection From Tricks

The clever believer in conjure does not wait until he or she gets tricked but takes precautions beforehand. There are a number of rituals and customs for this purpose, some of which might be classified as superstitious. Because they are directly aimed at preventing malefic conjure, however, they are treated as voodoo and hoodoo here.

Before these recipes are listed, note should be made of one of the ingredients that frequently occurs in them, and in other benefic conjure. It is High John the Conqueror root, High John the Conqueror powder, or Little John to Chew. High John the Conqueror is a Southern black folk character, most popular during slavery. It is said he came over from Africa, not as a slave but as a spirit, accompanying the slaves to help them retain their sense of humor and their sense of hope. He lived on the plantations unbeknownst to whites and at times would take the form of a slave. At such times, he would invariably have an "incident" with the master.

According to one of the many stories, he was working in a "big house" one time and got a taste for the roast pig the master enjoyed. So, he started stealing pigs and cooking them for himself in his shack in the quarters at night. The master started missing his pigs, suspected John, and late one night went to the quarters and made a surprise visit, just when John was roasting one of the master's pigs. When the master asked what was cooking that smelled so good, John replied, "Possum." The master decided he'd like some of that possum and John could not talk him out of it. Reluctantly, John lifted the lid of the roasting pot, looked at the master, and said, "Well, Massa, I put this thing in here a possum, but if it comes out a pig, it ain't no fault of mine." In spite of himself, the master had to laugh, and John got out of that one!

All the stories are funny; none are bitter or tragic. Whenever things got bad for the slaves, someone would remember how High John the Conqueror had outwitted the master and they would be able to laugh. When freedom came, it is said, John decided he might not be needed anymore, but he thought he'd stick around just in case. So he took up secret dwelling in a plant that grew all through the South, to wait and to provide, through the roots of that plant, help to his people when they needed it. The plant is Tormentil, whose strongly astringent roots are used in tanning, dyeing and medicine. Some aficianados had never obtained it except at a hoodoo drug store or spiritualist supply house and did not know what it was in nature.

Recall that one custom that has survived from the West African tradition is that of keeping a frizzled or curly-feathered hen in the yard, for she will scratch around all day and likely scratch up any conjure that has been buried there. In the absence of a hen, a switch—hickory, white oak, even grapevine—may be used to beat around and under the house to drive out the conjure. Or take a red onion and put some sulphur inside it by making a small hole in the onion and inserting the powder. Stick nine pins into the onion and place it under the left corner of your doorstep. A variation on this practice substitutes a ball of tinfoil for the onion and recommends hiding the ball at the north or east corner of the house.

An age-old custom among some in New Orleans and other southern cities is a daily scrubbing of the front steps with red brick dust, both to bring luck and to keep away evil. Others sprinkle urine around their steps, or throw it to the north side of the house as the sun comes up or to the south side as the sun goes down.

To protect the inside of the home, sprinkle red pepper and sulphur in all the corners to nullify the effect of any conjure hidden there. Burn incense. For this purpose there are uncrossing incense, jinx killer incense, drive away evil incense, and some cognoscenti simply specified white incense. These incenses may also be used in combination. Claude O. Winston, Jr., interviewed while shopping at the Dixie Drug Store, burns uncrossing incense and High John the Conqueror powder. *King Solomon's Guide* recommends a combination of items which cost, at this writing, $4.24:

§§ **Burn Grandma's Fast Luck Money Drawing incense and Luck in a Hurry incense and Drive Away Evil incense regularly. Wash your floor two or three times a week with Stop Evil Floor Wash.**

In addition to Stop Evil Floor Wash, a Jinx Remover wash is available. Another popular item for floor scrubbing is Van-Van oil.

Finally, protect your bed by spreading salt over the mattress before you put on the sheet.

With the home thus taken care of, both inside and outside, the next step for one who wishes to be thoroughly protected is to "dress" one's shoes. Sprinkle red pepper, salt, and sulphur in them before you put them on and any conjure you walk over will have no effect on you. Or take a dime and file it down and mix the filings with saltpeter and sprinkle that mixture in your shoes.

Another protective activity involving the shoes is to wear them on the opposite feet when you go out. You might also consider wearing your underclothing inside out. And two informants recommended putting nine drops of fresh turpentine into each shoe under the innersole.

You may also protect your bare feet. One practitioner who recommended burning incense to safeguard the house suggested that the feet be held over the smoke as a protection for the person, which seems an efficient way to accomplish two purposes with one activity. Mrs. M. in Montgomery supplied another protective barefoot activity:

§§ **Walk barefoot backwards out of your house nine steps. Do not look back. Then walk forward in the same tracks and when you reach your door, stop the tracks with a mixture of sugar, water and alcohol, or red pepper, saltpeter and brimstone [sulphur].**

To protect yourself further, wear a dime; some sources said it should be worn about the waist, others around the leg, to keep you from walking over conjure. And for extra added protection, cross two matches or two pins on your head.

Some initiates suggested chewing Little John to Chew whenever you venture away from your home. This is for general protection. If you suspect an attempt might be made to poison you, they suggest that you file a dime and put the dust in water and drink it. Any poison you eat or imbibe will not affect you as long as the silver is in your system, they say.

Mother W. supplied this formula for keeping major diseases away:

§§ **Tie a knotted rope around your waist. The knots are to be groupings of prayers similar to the rosary bead concept. One method is to 1) tie the first three knots reciting a "Hail Mary" as each knot is tied; 2) tie the next two knots reciting the "Glory be to the Father . . ."; 3) tie one knot reciting the Act of Contrition. Then repeat the procedure.**

Sometimes the groupings can be in threes, denoting Father, Son, and Holy Ghost. A "Hail Mary" is said as each knot is tied.

§§§ **Lucky Hands**

There are a great variety of items and "hands" to be carried for general protection and luck, and these have long been among the most successful items for hoodoo drug stores and mail order houses. The now defunct King Novelty Company in Chicago offered a number of them in its curio catalogues published in the 1950s, a sampling of which follows:

Southern Style Herb Bag dressed with Southern Style Van-Van Oil consisting of John the Conqueror, Adam and Eve Root (almost exclusively available at hoodoo supply houses), and lodestones in a red flannel bag and cost $1.00.

Novel Lodestone Fixed in a Bag with Lodestone Powder and Magnetic Sand consisted of two genuine magnetic lodestones specially selected to have magnetic power, with a generous supply of lodestone powder and magnetic sand. Flannel bag included. Price $1.00.

Alleged Mo-Jo Brand Lucky Curio Box—for drawing luck, getting jobs, winning in love, winning in gambling games. Contained Magnetic Lodestone, High John the Conqueror Root, 2 Adam and Eve Roots, and 1 vial of Van-Van Oil all in a red flannel bag. Price $1.00.

High John the Conqueror fixed in bag with Van-Van Oil and Five Finger Grass—to be worn around the neck and sprinkled every morning with two drops of Van-Van Oil—to drive away evil and attract money and luck. Price $1.00.

The Lucky Star Products Company in Columbus, Georgia, carries a Mr. Felix Special Lucky Hand ("Guaranteed Fast Results") that sells for $50.00, as well as an Extra Heavy Duty Lucky Hand ("When you need that extra Power. The Cadillac of Lucky Hands") for $100.00.

Dr. Sam offers a hand consisting of nine ingredients in the ubiquitous red flannel bag, among them Jerusalem bean (sold in hoodoo supply houses), devil's shoestring, High John the Conqueror root, bloodroot, snake root, and Adam and Eve root. Together, they cover every exigency from general protection to luck in love, business, and gambling.

According to Frank Hendricks, proprieter of the Dixie Drug Store, a similar general purpose hand can be made with Five Finger Grass alone, for each of its five parts is supposed to bring luck in a different area: wisdom, luck, power, love, and money. Another name for ginseng, Five Finger Grass is an appropriate common name for *Panax quinquefolius*.

Some practitioners recommend a mixture of graveyard dirt, steel dust, and pulverized High John the Conqueror root kept in a large bottle in the home, not carried on the person as are most "hands." Others feel you can dispense with both High John the Conqueror and graveyard dirt if you can obtain an eel skin to dry and pulverize and mix with steel dust in a red flannel bag. This can either be hidden in the home or carried on the person.

Almost as popular as the various "hands" in bags or boxes or bottles are the lucky bones, which are obtainable from commercial voodoo and hoodoo distributors. Purists prefer to obtain them from "scratch" as it were. Here are two involving frog bones:

§§   **Take a live frog and put him in a can of oil. Keep him there until the flesh separates easily from the bones. Then take the equivalent of a human collar bone or clavicle from the frog and carry it in your pocket.**

§§   **Take the left leg of a live frog and sew it up in a piece of chamois or red flannel. Tie it around your neck so that it hangs over your breast.**

And these two utilize human bones:

§§ Obtain from a dead man's grave the little finger bone from the left hand. Soak it in alcohol for nine days. Then take it back to the grave and bury it in the breast area. Pour sweet milk over the area for another nine days. Then dig it up and carry it in a red flannel bag. Sprinkle High John the Conqueror oil over it frequently.

§§ Obtain from the grave the corpse's knee bone. Wash it, dry it, and bleach it in the sun. Place it in a red flannel bag and carry it in your pocket.

Finally, here is how to get a lucky bone from a cat:

§§ Take a black cat and boil it until the flesh comes off the bones. Then take the bones to a stream or river and toss them in. The one that floats up stream is the lucky bone. Carry this lucky bone in your pocket.

Interestingly, the 7-African Powers Curio Shop in Houston carries an "Alleged Black Cat Bone" that is not from a cat at all but instead is "taken from a white chicken." Price is $3.00.

There is also a root that is actually shaped like a hand. King Novelty Company used to call this Salep root (a variation of the name Saloop.) To quote the catalogue:

§§ This is one of the most odd, weird looking Roots we have ever seen. It is uncanny in ap-

pearance and looks like a Human Hand. We have sold more of this Root than any other and we believe this is due to the Hand shape of the Root.

It was priced at 50¢ for a box of two roots.

Next to carrying hands for general luck or protection, the most frequent purpose of carrying a hand is luck in gambling. Gambling has traditionally been a way of life in poor black communities, as evidenced by the many successful Numbers operations and the large numbers of "Lucky Number Dream Books" that have been on the market for years. Understandably, people who are chronically unemployed or trapped in menial, low-paying jobs see gambling as one of the only ways to break out of the poverty cycle, and it is a common belief that if one gambles enough the odds are that he will eventually make that big score.

Some gamblers engage in rituals to bring luck in gambling. Here is a sampling:

§§ **Take a lodestone and some brimstone and go to the crossroads at midnight. Strike a match and light the brimstone, making it flare up. In that moment, a spirit (or a man, depending on the source) will come and give you advice as to when to play, when luck will be on your side, etc.**

§§ **Obtain some special rocks, usually called sea rocks, from the local hoodoo or spiritualist supply source. Light the rocks and they will smoke. Sprinkle some sugar and cinnamon on the rocks. Then pour it all over the gambler's shoes. Tell the gambler** to pass a coin over the shoes and wish for luck in gambling.

§§ Prepare a bag full of lodestone, cayenne, black pepper, and sugar. Put a live frog in with it and sprinkle some more cayenne pepper over it. It will jump. Every time you go out to gamble, sprinkle some more cayenne pepper into the bag. The frog will die in time, but for the period he lives you will be extremely lucky.

Here's what *King Solomon's Guide* advises for luck in gambling, specifically, to make your right hand lucky. At this writing, ingredients cost $5.67:

§§ 2 Conquering soaps, liquid
   1 Money soap, liquid
   2 bottles of Sonny Boy's Special Oil
   1 bottle of Jinx Killer oil

Just before you get into the game or buy tickets, wash the right hand in Conquering soap with the left hand. Then wash both hands with the Money soap. Then put three drops of Jinx Killer oil on your hands and rub them until they are hot. Next put nine drops of Sonny Boy's Special Oil in the palms. After this your luck will be good.

And here is a prescription calculated to help you win money playing the Numbers as well as generally drawing money to you. Each prescription in the "Guide" is given in the context

of an anecdote. Here the anecdote is included.
Ingredients cost $6.23:

§§ **Ted said that he is always winning money. I
asked him what did he use for luck and he said.**

> 2 **Winning Number Incenses**
> 2 **Jinx Killer Oil**
> 3 **Grandma's Lucky Hand Oil**

**I anoint my body with Jinx Killer Oil to keep the
jinx off me. I use Lucky Hand Oil all the time to
keep drawing money to yourself. I asked does it
work? Ted said I'm satisfied with the results. I said
you did not tell me what to do with the Winning
Number Incenses and he said burn man, it is a sure
winner.**

Most serious gamblers dispense with such
rituals and just carry "gambling hands," which
can be combinations of a variety of items.
Some gamblers prefer to make their own, but
many gambling hands are available ready-
made from hoodoo drugstores and mail-order
houses. Among the most popular hands are
those that include High John the Conqueror in
some form.

§§ **Take High John the Conqueror, devil's shoestring, lodestone, magnetic sand and dragon's teeth
powder (available at hoodoo supply stores). Place
these ingredients in a bag made of chamois. Sprinkle lucky oil in and on the bag. Carry it with you
whenever you gamble.**

§§ Place High John the Conqueror, devil's shoe-string, a dime and a piece of lodestone in a red flannel bag. Soak it in urine (if you have a wife or girlfriend, her urine is best) until you go out gambling. Then carry it in your pocket. As long as the bag remains wet, you will be lucky so it is necessary to soak it, (sometimes called feeding) with some frequency.

A red onion is also a common basis for a gambling hand:

§§ Steal a red onion—it will not be lucky if you pay for it. Make a small hole in the onion and put cayenne and sulphur in it. Wrap it tightly in a bag made of red flannel or chamois and soak it either in lucky oil or John the Conqueror perfume. Carry it with you when you go gambling, and just before you start, rub your hands on the bag.

§§ Obtain a red onion (legally, it is presumed) and make nine holes in it. Put nine pins in the holes and fill the holes up with sulphur. Wrap the onion in a piece of flannel and carry it in your pocket when you go gambling.

And many gamblers swear by their lucky bones. Some carry black cat bones, which are obtained and used for gambling luck just as they are for general luck and protection. Others prefer human bones:

§§ Obtain a finger bone from a grave (presumably because the fingers do most of the work in card playing, dice throwing and even in shooting pool. Also, the finger bones are small and fit nicely into pockets). Bleach the bone white in the sun and carry it when you go gambling, rubbing it frequently for luck. The more you rub it, the smoother and shinier it becomes.

Other people carry lucky stones, which they dress with various money-drawing oils and perfumes, and one source recommended carrying a live frog (no doubt because, being green, a frog has a certain affinity with money) and rubbing it frequently while gambling.

Money is a very necessary ingredient of the good life, and there are a number of potions and hands and procedures calculated to draw money, but not necessarily through gambling. Claude O. Winston, Jr., interviewed in the Dixie Drug Store, said burning green candles and money-drawing incense worked for him. Joseph Bush, an employee at the store, uses money-drawing oil. "There are several customers who use the oil," he says. "They've come back and told me that it worked for them; some rewarded me for telling them what to use." Bush shoots pool. "I've been using the oil about ten years," he says, "and I've been winning." The Dixie Drug Store carries a large variety of money-drawing perfumes, oils, incenses, and powders.

King Solomon's Guide gives the following prescription under the heading "Can You Be Lucky And Get Money Quick?" Ingredients at this writing cost $4.91.

§§   Quick Money Oil
     Jinx Killer Oil
     Uncrossing Power Oil
     Make Your Wish Oil
     Stop Evil Floor Wash

Mix Quick Money Oil, Jinx Killer Oil, Uncrossing
Power Oil, and Make Your Wish Oil. Hide this
mixture where no one knows where it is but you.
Wash your floors twice a week with Stop Evil Floor
Wash in your scrub water. Put about half a bottle in
each time you wash the floor.

§§§   Luck in Business

There are many prescriptions calculated to
bring success or to aid legitimate money-getting
enterprises. Here are some prescriptions and
rituals for getting a job:

§§   Use a red onion in a way similar to its use for
other types of luck. Either have it dressed by a
hoodoo practictioner or dress it yourself by boring a
hole in it and filling the hole with sulphur. Carry it
in your pocket when you go to the prospective
employer and squeeze it as you speak to him. (He
may give you the job just to get you out of the room.)

§§   Take a small piece of red flannel and put three
needles on it, side by side. Wrap the flannel and
needles in a piece of thread. Place them in a bag
made of yellow homespun. Carry the bag when you
go for your interview and you will get the job.

§§   Before going to the interview place three grains of salt in a handkerchief and put it in your pocket. When you get to the place of employment, wait until you are alone or the interviewer is somehow distracted. Then throw the salt into the north corner of the room. Within three days you will have the job.

§§   Read the thirty-fifth Psalm (which seems rather extreme for this purpose as it deals primarily with enemies. However, the first line may be operative: "Plead my cause, O Lord ...") for nine mornings before seeking the job. Carry High John the Conqueror root in your pocket and rub your body with success oil.

King Solomon's Guide gives the following prescriptions, whose ingredients cost at this writing, $9.79:

§§   2 Luck in a Hurry incenses
     2 Luck in a Hurry oils
     3 Steady Work incenses
     2 Steady Work oils
     2 Fast Luck Money Drawing incenses

Mix together all three incenses. Burn three table-spoons full of incenses with a few drops of Luck in a Hurry Oil and Steady Work Oil twice a day. Carry the Steady Work Oil with you and anoint yourself just before you apply for a job.

§§ A job-getting hand may be made by obtaining a lodestone and sprinkling steel filings on it (to draw a person to you). Place it in a red flannel bag and wear it next to your heart. When you go to the interview, look the man straight in the eye and concentrate on getting the job.

If you want to take in roomers or rent your house, these prescriptions are supposed to help:

§§ To attract roomers, get some powdered High John the Conqueror root and some powdered love vine (available at hoodoo supply stores). Mix it in a bottle of success perfume. Put three drops at the front door and back door and at the door of each room you want occupied. Also scrub your front steps with it. The roomers will come unbidden.

§§ To rent your house, wash it thoroughly with an appropriate oil—Magnet Oil, Three Sisters Oil, Fast Success Oil, depending on the practitioner—in your scrub water. Then take the scrub water and go out the back of the house a few steps away. Throw the water over your left shoulder. Don't look back. You will hardly have hung up your "For Rent" sign when you will have a tenant.

§§ To rent your house, scrub your house at sunrise with brown sugar, ammonia, and drawing oil. While you are scrubbing, burn drawing incense. You will soon have your house rented.

There are numerous ways to attract customers to your place of business.

§§   In New Orleans it is believed that Saint Peter governs business because he carries the keys. Get up early in the morning and light a white candle to Saint Peter. Then mix green herbs into your scrub water—especially parsley and thyme. Begin scrubbing from the front of your place of business and work toward the back, moving backwards as you go. When you reach the back, burn green incense there. All of these measures are calculated to "draw" customers.

§§   This ritual can be accomplished in your home rather than in your business place. Get up early and burn a mixture of sulphur and sugar and appropriate incense, usually the controlling or compelling kind. As the sun rises, look to the East and pray for customers to be drawn to you.

§§   Go to the graveyard and get nine handfuls of dirt. Back home, mix it with brimstone, sulphur, red pepper, and salt. Burn the mixture and pray for success in business.

§§   Go to your place of business before sunrise nine mornings in a row. As the sun comes up, touch the ground in front of your establishment and ask God to bring customers to that spot.

A number of informants suggested putting various lucky hands dressed with money-drawing oils right inside the cash register or money drawer, thereby compelling customers in the store to buy something before they leave. Such hands included the usual ingredients, such as High John the Conqueror root, and did not differ measurably from the hands recently described and to be described later.

Finally, here is the oddest method for drawing customers that I encountered. It was supplied by an initiate in Birmingham, Alabama:

§§ Obtain the shoe of the oldest woman you can find. Take it to your place of business and burn it. This is calculated to drive away bad business. Then, obtain on a piece of clean cloth some of the first menstrual blood of a very young girl. Put the cloth over your door. This is to attract new business.

§§§ A Benefic Miscellany

To make someone do your bidding or to gain power over someone:

§§ Mix together sulphur and brimstone and put it in a box. Put seven pins, heads up, in it. Carry it in your pocket and when you encounter the person you have in mind, squeeze the box and you will control him.

§§ Put pulverized Adam and Eve Root in a small bottle with either whiskey or Controlling Power perfume. Before you address the person you wish to control, daub this mixture on your face three times a day.

To guarantee peace and happiness:

§§   Take powdered dragon's blood and mix it with sugar and salt in a bottle or box. Cover it and hide it. As long as no one discovers it, you will have peace.

§§   Burn white candles constantly in your home.

Mother W. supplied two formulas to ensure safety.

§§   To stop lightning from striking your house, light a broom straw and throw it outside.

§§   To ensure the safety of your child, cut a lock of its hair when it is a baby and keep it with you. The child must have all of its hair before it can die.

According to Mother W., during the Civil War a great deal of money and other valuables were buried in Louisiana by Southerners who wished to keep the Yankees from getting it. Many people still dig in hopes of finding treasure that was never recovered.

§§   Take precautions before you go out to dig for buried treasure. You must wait for a full moon, and you must get to the spot before midnight in order to avoid meeting up with the dead spirits that go out at midnight. Wear a rosary and cross around your neck or else the more you dig the deeper the money will sink.
Many people bury a dead animal (usually a cat)

**with the money to protect it. The dead animal will
rise when you start digging, and you must stare it
directly in the eye or it will kill you. Then, you can
get the money.**

Although it is hard to imagine this problem
occuring with any measurable frequency, there
might be times when steps must be taken to
keep unwanted persons out of your car. *King
Solomon's Guide* gives the following prescription. Cost of ingredients at this writing: $3.56.

§§ **Sprinkle Cast Off Evil incense on the floor mat
of your car. Bury three containers of Spiritual
Power incense in your yard. Read the twenty-
seventh Psalm for nine mornings.**

Finally, voodoo dolls may be used for benefic
as well as evil purposes. For those who do not
care to make their own, the Mi-World Bookstore in Hialeah, Florida, carries red dolls for
love and romance, pink dolls for success and
attraction, green dolls for luck and money, and
yellow dolls for dispelling evil. Like the black
doll (cure, hate, evil), they are handmade of
cloth, about six inches tall, packaged with
name tag, pin, cord, and description of How to
Voodoo with Dolls, and cost $5.00 each.

VI

In Matters of Law

There is a substantial body of hoodoo, voodoo, and spiritualist lore involving crime and the law. Often called "Court Spells" by folklorists, the majority of the conjures concern the circumventing of legal sanctions by means of conjuration. These have changed with the times. In the days of slavery, potions and hands to help escaped slaves avoid capture or to prevent bloodhounds from picking up a runaway's scent were prevalent. During Prohibition there were a number of prescriptions and devices aimed specifically at "Revenuers" and to protect bootleggers; and when capital punishment was more common there were a greater number of methods for dealing with the various means by which capital punishment is rendered. But people still have trouble with the law, and so there are still many "Court Spells."

§§§ Bringing a Murderer to Justice

One area that has not changed essentially over the years is that concerning the identification and bringing to justice of murderers. It is an age-old and widespread belief that if the suspect is made to touch the corpse, the corpse will respond to the touch of the murderer's hand, and that even if the body is cold and rigor mortis has set in, blood will somehow spurt from the victim's mouth or from the wound in response to the touch of the guilty party.

As a child, I heard of another method of identifying a murderer—one involving a victim's grave:

§§   Obtain a shoe worn by a baby less than a year old—a girl's or boy's, depending on the gender of the victim. Dig down toward the place of the victim's heart, as deep as possible without actually touching the coffin or other encasement of the body. Take a handful of the dirt from the bottom of the hole and put it into the baby shoe. At midnight burn the shoe and call upon the spirit of the victim to bring the murderer back. Then carry the ashes back to the grave and bury them in another hole in the middle of the ground above the grave. In a matter of days the murderer will identify himself in some way.

The reason for using a baby's shoe here is the comparative ease of controlling a baby's mind. It is an ancient black belief, rooted in Africa, that a baby has an undeveloped mind, and thus one that is easily controlled. A similar belief has long been held about the mind of a sleeping adult.

If the problem is not identification but apprehension of the murderer, there are several methods by which he can be caused to return.

None of my sources had ever been personally called upon to use, or witnessed the employment of, these methods (or would not admit to it) but they were familiar with them. Mrs. M. in Montgomery and Dr. K. in New Orleans supplied the following prescriptions:

§§ **To bring a murderer back, go to the grave of the victim at night and move the headstone to the area of the feet. Take some of the dirt from the head area of the grave and when you get home mix it with sulphur, red pepper, and brimstone. Burn that mixture and the murderer will be compelled to return.**

§§ **The corpse can help to bring back the murderer. As soon after death as possible, take an egg laid by a black hen and write the name of the murderer on the egg nine times. Put the egg in the palm of the corpse's right hand and close the fingers around it, if possible. The murderer will return by the time of the funeral.**

Several other informants also mentioned the use of eggs to compel a murderer to return. A similar but more elaborate prescription than Dr. K's is this:

§§ **Obtain three eggs from a black hen. Put one in each of the victim's hands and one behind his neck. Place an open pair of scissors on his chest to form a cross (or X) of steel. Then close the hands on the eggs to crush them and lift up on the head to crush the other egg. The murderer will soon return.**

Another means of bringing back a murderer, mentioned by several sources, is to obtain an item of the murderer's clothing and bury it in the grave with the victim. Thus symbolically joined to the victim through the operation of the principle of like-to-like, the murderer is compelled to come back to the place where the crime was committed.

Finally, a nonpractitioner in Birmingham mentioned a case involving, literally, the writing on the wall. She could not remember clearly if the wall in question was in the victim's home or the murderer's home, but she rather thought it was the victim's, and that is more likely. A local hoodoo doctor was employed by the victim's family to bring the murderer back, and every night for nine nights at nine o'clock the doctor wrote the murderer's name on the wall. By the tenth day the murderer had been apprehended by the police.

§§§   How a Murderer Avoids Justice

If the murderer has his wits about him, of course he takes precautions against such spiritual law enforcement. According to Dr. Sam, a lot has to do with what he does when, in the course of his escape, he comes to a crossroads. If he does not want to be followed, he can take two sticks, one long and one short, and cross them, pointing the longer stick in the direction opposite the direction he intends to go. If he does not want to be compelled to return, he must bury the two sticks, wrapping his handkerchief or a scrap of his clothing around the longer stick. In this way he uses the principle of like-to-like for his own benefit, for no power can make him return when, by virtue of the presence of the buried item, he has never left. Another crossroads practice that a fugitive can employ is this:

§§ **When you reach the crossroads, select the road you will take. Then walk backwards a few steps (usually nine, but one source specified twelve) in the opposite direction. Your pursuer will take that wrong road.**

Some of my sources stated flatly that a murderer could not do hoodoo, but Dr. Sam is not the only one who disagrees. A source in North Carolina told how a woman who knew a lot about the art avoided conviction for murder by breaking two eggs over her left shoulder.

§§§ **Avoiding the Law**

Eggs enjoy considerable importance in conjure to avoid the law or prosecution. Usually, but not always, the names of the parties concerned are written on them. For example, if you are visited by two policemen who wish to question you and you have a feeling you might be arrested, you find out their names. Write their names on the eggs and break the eggs on your roof. The police will not return.

Mrs. S. of Charleston did a similar thing for a

client whose husband was up for trial and for whom conviction would have resulted in a prison sentence. Mrs. S. obtained several eggs from a pure white chicken. On them she wrote the names of the judge, prosecuting attorney, and prosecution witnesses. The night before the trial was to begin she drove to the courthouse and at midnight tossed the eggs up onto the building's roof. They broke. The next day her client happily informed her that plea bargaining had taken place and that her husband had received a suspended sentence.

These various prescriptions employing eggs serve to illustrate the long-held belief that most items or ingredients are equally powerful for good or evil. They are shown in these prescriptions to be as powerful in upholding the law as in subverting it.

Several instances were given of chewing roots or seeds while before a judge or the police. The most frequently mentioned root was the faithful and versatile High John the Conqueror, called in such cases Little John to Chew because small pieces are sold specifically for chewing purposes. Little else is needed besides this extremely powerful root. A more complicated ritual involves the chewing of guinea seed (seeds from hot, or guinea, peppers) by the defendant while someone at home simultaneously cooks red kidney beans, which are lucky:

§§ **Not only must you chew the guinea seed, but you must spit liberally as well, getting bits of the seed all around the courtroom. The pot of red kidney beans being cooked in the meantime must** contain a piece of paper on which has been written the judge's name three times and your name nine times. There must be no other seasoning, for the presence of the paper keeps the judge's mind on you and your case. When you go before him he is primed to hear your side, and the power of the guinea seed helps ensure a favorable verdict.

Another "chewing conjure" involves Wish Beans, unshelled peanut-like beans sold in hoodoo supply houses. Obtained from a practitioner in Louisiana, this method involves considerable preparation beforehand, utilizing candles and other items.

§§ Mix together the dried root of High John the Conqueror, dried Dragon Blood, and dried Dove's Blood. Hide them in parchment paper in the farthest corners of your home. Write the names of your friends and allies on nine pieces of paper and set them under nine black candles. Burn one brown and one black candle side by side each day, but far enough apart so the waxes will not mix.

On the day your case comes up for trial, take Wish Beans with you. Chew them constantly, and drop the hulls about you. The judge will be inclined to listen to you and your friends rather than to your enemies and prosecutors.

One practitioner mentioned Law Turning powder and Get Away powder, both of which, he said, could be obtained through the usual channels. Law Turning powder is to be sprinkled around the house, ending a distance from the door. Thereafter you walk nine steps toward the door and sprinkle the powder in the ninth track, grinding it into the dirt with your foot. No officer of the law will be able to go beyond that point. Get Away powder is rubbed on the soles of the shoes and scattered as the first nine steps are taken from the point of departure. This author has not found powders bearing such names in catalogues or drug stores contacted, although the 7-African Powers Curio Shop in Houston stocks a Law Stay Away sprinkle, which is probably similar to Law Turning Powder. Among other hoodoo supply sources, the Dixie Drug Store does carry a seal, to be affixed somewhere around the home or to the door, called The Seal of Mystical Assistance in Disputes at Law and at Play.

King Solomon's Alledged Guide to Success? Power! prescribes a suitably complex and costly (at this writing ingredients cost $20.16) method of avoiding trouble with the law:

§§   **Sonny Boy's Luck in a Hurry incenses and oil**
     4 **Sonny Boy's Seven Holy Spirits salt**
     7 **Sonny Boy's Drive Away Evil incenses**
     4 **bottles Old Indian clear water**
       Sonny Boy's Indian spray

Bury the four bottles of Old Indian clear water in your yard, with he tops pointed away from the house—one on the east side of the house, one on the west, one on the north, and one on the south. Pour one container of Seven Holy Spirits salt on each of the bottles and cover them up. Spray the house with Indian spray. Bury Drive Away Evil incenses in your yard. Burn Luck in a Hurry incenses three times a week as long as you need this protection.

And yet it would appear that a similar result can be obtained in a much less costly manner, provided one has access to hickory root.

§§ **Take some hickory root and burn it to ashes. Mix these ashes with some blueing (laundry) powder. Put the mixture in a small box or other small container and place it over your door.**

Not exactly an example of the principle of like-to-like, this is nevertheless related, for the blueing is used here to keep *blue uniformed* police officers away.

Dr. T. in New Orleans remembered hearing of another method fo keeping the law away, although he could not say if the practice continued:

§§ **Obtain a beef tongue and two ice cubes and wrap them in a piece of white silk, the tongue between the ice cubes. Hide it somewhere so it will not be disturbed.**

Dr. T. declined to comment on the reasoning behind this practice. Assumedly, the purpose of the ice cubes is to freeze the tongue and thus symbolically to prevent anyone from telling the cops on the person in question.

Another symbolic practice, but one that is not used with much frequency because of the necessity of admitting the would-be captors or arresters, is to boil snails and put some of the water in which the snails boiled into the food or drink you serve the enemy. Once they have ingested this snail water, they will be unable to pursue you at a rate any faster than "a snail's pace."

An informant in South Carolina also gave a prescription for keeping the law off one's back that necessitated being around the prospective pursuer.

§§ **Follow him, or them, until you are able to obtain some of the dirt from the heel of their left foot print and some from the toe of their right foot print. Then go to the grave of your most recently deceased friend or acquaintance and obtain some of the dirt from the grave, explaining to the corpse's spirit why you are taking the dirt. Back home, obtain the blood from a black animal—cat, sheep, or chicken—available in many hoodoo stores; heat it and mix the foot print dirt, the graveyard dirt and the blood together. Spread the mixture in front of both your front and your back doors at dawn and read the twenty-first Psalm while doing so.**

The operative verses in this Psalm are probably: "For they intended evil against thee: they imagined a mischievous device, which they are not able to perform./Therefore shalt thou make them turn their backs . . ." Religion, as has been mentioned before, can be an integral part of hoodoo as well as voodoo. My sources in New Orleans were more likely to couch their work in religious terms than were those in other parts of the country, but all of my informants professed a deep respect for the power of God and His hand in their work.

§§§   How to Win a Lawsuit

There are also a number of practices designed to bring about a positive resolution of a lawsuit in which one is involved, whether it be civil or criminal. Here are two that call upon the help of the twelve Apostles—an obvious association, considering that a jury is composed of twelve persons:

§§   **Take two pieces of paper and write the names of six Apostles on each. Put one paper, folded, in each shoe and when you go into court the matter at hand will be decided in your favor.**

This one distinguishes Judas from the others and substitutes another appropriate biblical personage.

§§   **Obtain twelve sage leaves. Write the names of all the Apostles except Judas on eleven of them and put them in either one of your shoes. On the twelfth sage leaf write the name of the biblical personage most appropriate to your case: for example, if you are accused of murder write the name Cain because Cain slew Abel. If you do not know an appropriate name, leave the twelfth leaf blank. Put it in your other shoe. So armed when you go to trial, you will be acquitted.**

And this one uses Judas' name positively:

§§   **Take one piece of paper and write the names of five Apostles on one side and six Apostles on the** other. Fold it and put in in your right shoe. Write the name of the twelfth Apostle—Judas is best—on a second piece of paper and put it in your left shoe. Because you have "divided" the twelve Apostles in this manner, the jury will be divided on your case. They will be unable to reach a verdict, and no matter how many times your case is tried there will be a hung jury or a mistrial every time.

Speaking of "hung juries," I encountered one conjure practice, and undoubtedly there are more, that involves like-to-like, or hanging an object to cause a hung jury.

§§ Go to the market and buy a beef tongue. Write the names of the members of the jury (or of the witnesses against you, or of the judge, prosecuting attorney and witnesses against you, depending on the source) on a piece of parchment paper. Make a hole in the tip of the tongue and place the paper in the hole. Hang the tongue over a hot fire or have someone do it for you and go to court. There will be a hung jury.

And to "freeze" the mouths of those who would testify against you:

§§ Write the names of your opponent, his witnesses, and his lawyer on a piece of parchment paper. Place it between two bricks. On the day of the trial set a bucket full of ice on top of the bricks and your opponents will be unable to testify against you.

The ingredients for an appropriate prescription in *King Solomon's Alledged Guide to Success? Power!* cost, at this writing, only $3.13. Here is the anecdote in which the prescription is presented:

§§ **Mary said that she had some troubles and was faced with a serious law suit. I asked her what she do. She said she burned Fast Success incenses and Compelling Power incenses every day. Pronounce the Holy name Ja several times, then rub "OLD INDIAN" CLEAR WATER over the face. Make your wish and ask that it be granted in the Name of the Lord. Amen. I ask her how did she make out, and she said she won the case.**

The Mi-World Bookstore sells a Success in Court Kit for $5.00:

This kit contains jalap powder, snakehead root, John the Conqueror root, and all instructions that will aid you. This will give you confidence in going into court. (Jalop is a dry, tuberous root.)

And the 7-African Powers Curio Shop in Houston stocks several items that are appropriate to this discussion, among them: XX (Double-Strength) Court Case Candle, brown with red key; Court Case Candle, Court Case Oil, and Court Water to wear at court, in addition to the aforementioned Law Stay Away sprinkle.

§§§   How to Get Out of Jail

Some people, of course, manage to find themselves in jail before they turn to a spirtualist or
hoodoo practitioner for help. In many cases it is
still not too late. Some conjure is powerful
enough to get a prisoner out of jail.

§§   The conjurer goes to a graveyard and obtains
nine handfuls of dirt from a fresh grave. The dirt
should be gotten from an area about a foot and a
half from the headstone. It is combined with sulphur, red pepper, and brimstone. Then the conjurer,
or the prisoner's spouse if available, burns that
mixture in the prisoner's home. In a short time the
prisoner is released, although the circumstances
leading to his release may vary considerably.

A source in South Carolina told of a practice
among more rural folk.

§§   Obtain about seven pieces of root from a myrtle
bush. Boil this red root until it turns white. Dry the
root and pulverize most of it, but save some. Go to
the graveyard and get some dirt from a fresh grave.
Mix that with the pulverized root. Visit the prisoner
in jail. As you walk through the jailhouse to the cell,
sprinkle the powder along the way. While with the
prisoner, give him a piece of the dry, whole root to
chew. Thenceforth, whenever the prisoner speaks
with the jailer, his attorney, or anyone else connected with his case, he must chew the root. Once
again the circumstances vary, but shortly the prisoner is freed.

The final method for getting a person out of jail presented here was obtained in New Orleans and involves, among other things, the burning of candles. This method appears to apply in a case where an appeal is pending or a new trial has been ordered:

§§   Take green and yellow candles, enough to last for nine days, and with a sharp object write on them the names of the chief prosecution witness, the judge, and the district attorney, in that order. Burn the candles upside down to "upset the heads" of these people. Bore a hole in each of three apples and put the name of each of the three above-mentioned persons in the apples. Set them before the candles while they burn the requisite nine days. At the end of nine days take the apples to the vicinity of the jail. Roll one from the entrance, one from the right side, and one from the left side, thereby rolling the prisoner out of jail.

§§§   Miscellaneous Court Conjure

Under what might be termed *Miscellaneous* are the various methods to recover stolen items:

§§   Go to the graveyard and wake up the spirit of a deceased relative or friend by moving the headstone of his grave and calling his name three times. Ask the spirit to trouble the mind of the person who has stolen from you and place three pennies on the head of the grave as payment. (It is a common belief that spirits do not do something for nothing.) The thief will be tormented until he returns to you what he stole.

§§ Buy a new pair of white socks or stockings and wear them for nine days. For the next nine mornings snap them quickly over a fire, just enough to scorch them slightly. By the tenth morning the stolen item will be returned.

§§ Take nine horseshoe nails and nail them into your doorsill (if you have a wooden one), all the while calling out the name of the stolen item and ordering it back. If it is still in the possession of the thief (the conjure does not appear to work on "fences") and intact, it will be returned.

King Solomon's Alledged Guide to Success? Power! recommends the following procedure for recovering stolen money. At this writing, ingredients cost $6.23.

§§ 2 Compelling Power incense
    2 Spiritual Power incense
    2 Fast Luck Money Drawing
    1 Fast Luck Money Drawing oil

Burn half a box of Compelling Power incense and half a box of Fast Luck Money Drawing incense. Put Spiritual Power incense behind your door and read the seventy-seventh Psalm. The thief will be identified to you in a vision. Continue to burn Compelling Power for three days. The thief will return the money.

The seventy-seventh Psalm does not address the matter of theft directly, but it does ask the Lord's help in trouble.

In New Orleans one commonly prays to Saint Raymond (for favors) for this purpose. Pray to him for nine days, give him appropriate reimbursement for his trouble, and on the ninth day your property will be returned.

On the other hand there are ways to protect yourself if you desire to steal and not get caught or be forced to pay for what you have taken. This method was supplied by Mrs. S. in Charleston:

§§ **Obtain a live chicken and split open its breast. Take a length of blue silk long enough to fit around your waist and dip it into the open breast cavity. Tie the bloody cloth around your waist, and you may take anything—from a store or from a friend—and not risk capture or being forced to pay.**

Finally, under the category of Court Miscellany is the recollection of an informant in South Carolina. Though presented by the source as an example of conjure, it is more appropriate in the category of *con*. It is said that true voodoo and hoodoo practitioners have a keen understanding of psychology, and nowhere is this skill better demonstrated than in the following anecdote:

§§ **A woman saddled with a mountain of debts was sued by one of her creditors for nonpayment. Desperate, she went to a hoodoo practitioner for help. The doctor told her to enter the court borne on a stretcher. Accordingly, she arranged for two men to carry her before the judge in this manner. The judge refused to find her guilty.**

§§§ VII

In Matters of Love

"I live on a big Virginian plantation, and some five or six negro families have their cabins near the big house, numbering in all, including pickaninnies, about thirty-five people," wrote a white contributor to the *Journal of American Folk-Lore* in December 1896. "At the beginning of this year, a likely young gingerbread darkey was hired to wait about the house and drive the carriage . . .

"Tom is the boy's name, and as soon as he became domesticated in his new home he began to pay attention to one of the dusky lassies on the place. Susan was much pleased at the notice . . . But suddenly, for some reason, Tom cooled off and began to cast sheep's eyes at another girl. Susan lost her high spirits and became gloomy and dejected . . .

"Presently . . . a change came over him also, and he complained of being sick and having 'a misery.' Tom had been taking his meals in the kitchen where Susan's mother is cook, and we supposed he feared the old cook would trick him, as he requested his mistress to give him rations. . . . One morning, about a month ago, Tom did not come to his work at the usual time, and later in the day he sent word by another negro that he was sick and had gone to see a doctor; he returned in a day or two, but looked thin and badly, and he soon said that the place did not agree with him and he would go off for a change and try to get better.

"He was off for ten days, and about a week ago he returned, looking much better, and he said he was now all right. . . . But he soon seemed downcast and drooping again, and two days ago he came to see his mistress and told her he would have to leave, that he had no health here, and could never have any, as 'somebody had given him some nasty pizen stuff that made him sick.' He left last night and has not returned . . ."

Just as "love makes the world go round," so has it accounted for a substantial amount of conjure, and over the centuries the area of "love conjure" appears to have changed remarkably little among blacks in the New World. Love potions, devices to keep a man at home or a woman happy or to get revenge still make up a large portion of voodoo and hoodoo lore, and support a goodly number of hoodoo, voodoo, and spiritualist practitioners. Female root workers still seem to exercise a certain monopoly on the market, although most male practitioners can prescribe similar formulas. As with other types of conjure, the basic changes over the years have concerned the paraphernalia of the conjure and the ingredients of the formulas. For example, Hurston reported that a New Orleans practitioner in the late 1920s prescribed the following rite for a woman who wanted to make a man love her:

§§ **Turn down the sweat band in his hat and pin two needles in it, across each other.**

With the decreased popularity of hats and the frequent absence of sweat bands in hat styles that are favored, such a practice has diminished.

In earlier times, romantic spells were generally conducted either at the full of the moon or at he dark of the moon, or when the moon was beginning to rise. Nowadays, with the popularity of astrology, there is more concern with the "planetary hours, when the moon is waxing and the Venus hours are most conducive." According to Charles M. Gandolfo, proprieter of the Voodoo Museum, the following are the most favorable hours:

Sunday	2:00 and 9:00 A.M.	4:00 and 11:00 P.M.
Monday	6:00 A.M.	1:00 and 8:00 P.M.
Tuesday	3:00 and 10:00 A.M.	5:00 and 12:00 P.M.
Wednesday	7:00 A.M.	2:00 and 9:00 P.M.
Thursday	4:00 and 11:00 A.M.	6:00 P.M.
Friday	1:00 and 8:00 A.M.	7:00 P.M.

§§§   How to Attract a Man or Woman

There are lots of ways to attract a member of the opposite sex or to draw that person to you. Here's how to attract a man:

§§   Obtain a lock of his hair and wrap it in a small piece of cloth, folding the cloth toward you. Put it in the bottom of your shoe and he will come to you.

§§   Make a mixture of orange flower water, rose water, and honey. Add to this nine lumps of sugar on each of which you have written his name first and then yours. Burn a pink candle in this mixture every day for nine days.

§§   Take some underarm and pubic hair and grind it up with fresh coffee. Brew it by the drip method, sweeten it liberally and serve it to him when he comes to call. He will fall in love with you.

And there are also specific prescriptions for attracting a woman:

§§   Make a potion of hoodoo oil, High John the Conqueror root, and Adam and Eve oil. (Some sources say hoodoo oil already includes the other two ingredients.) Put some of it on a handkerchief and carry it with you. Get close enough to her so she will smell it. Or, to make extra sure, get playful and snap her with the handkerchief. She will follow you from that time on.

§§   Take a lodestone and place it in a piece of red flannel. Sprinkle some Hearts Cologne and some of your urine on it. Carry it in your pocket until you encounter the woman. Then rub your hand on the lodestone and touch her with that hand. She will do anything you want.

§§   Take a piece of writing paper and dip all four corners first in Hearts Cologne and then in your urine. Then, starting at the lower left corner and proceeding to the upper right, write her name backwards, so it will be coming toward you. Put the paper in an envelope and send it to her. She will be yours as soon as she receives it.

Methods that apply to both men and women include the following:

§§   Bathe your feet to soften the dry skin thereon. Scrape off some of the dry skin and heat it until it is dry enough to be powdered. Put it in any beverage and give it to the person to drink. The person will then follow you all the time.

§§   Obtain a sample of the person's handwriting, preferably in ink. Sprinkle the paper with Wishing Oil and wear it next to your heart for nine days. Then bury it under your door step. After that any request you put in writing to that person will be granted. Ask him or her to be yours and you will have your way.

§§   Obtain a piece of the person's hair and sprinkle some Controlling Powder on it. Fold it toward you in a piece of white linen and wrap that, toward you once again, with blue (for true love) silk thread.

Carry it with you and you will have control over the person's mind. He or she will follow you and do whatever you wish.

Finally, *King Solomon's Alledged Guide to Success? Power!* prescribes the following for causing someone to love you. At this writing, total cost of ingredients at the Dixie Drug Store was $9.98.

§§ 2 Jinx Killer incense and oil
2 Love Drawing Power bath
2 Strong Love cologne
2 Make Your Wish sand

Dig a hole about one foot deep in your front yard, pour Make Your Wish sand into it and cover up the hole with dirt. Use the Jinx Killer incense and oil according to directions on package. Anoint yourself with Strong Love cologne two times a day for three weeks. Put Love Drawing Power bath in your bath water for twelve baths. Success will be achieved in the third week.

§§§ To Keep Your Man True

Once marriage or a marriage-like arrangement occurs, however, such potions and hands no longer appear to exercise power. New prescriptions are needed to deal with the crises and situations that develop in cohabitative arrangements.

The major portion of the trade of many female root workers involves prescribing methods to married women who wish to keep their men at home and to keep young, unmarried women from taking their husbands. Here are two methods for keeping the men at home:

§§ Scrape some of the dry skin from his heel when he is sleeping. Bury it under the doorstep. He will be unable to go out on you.

§§ Take one of your own belts, one that you wear frequently, and tie it to a nearby tree. The nearer the tree is to your home the better, for once that belt is tied around it your husband will be able to stray no farther than the tree.

And Mother W. in New Orleans offered this method:

§§ Cut off a lock of the man's hair while he is sleeping, but make sure he is sleeping on the left side of the bed. Take the lock of hair and some sassafras and put them in a small piece of cloth. Tie the loose ends of the cloth with a foot-long string by wrapping the string around it three times. Tie three knots on the end of the string and say a "Hail Mary" as you tie each knot. Then put the bag under the front steps, and the man will remain faithful.

Now if the husband suddenly finds himself prevented from going out and meeting other women, he naturally suspects that his wife has put some spell on him, in which case he must go to a *male* practitioner to have the spell removed. In some areas this can mean a long journey, but the husband willingly makes the trip for relief. He would not dare go to a woman for gender loyalties are strictly defined in his town, and he would not risk incurring her enmity. Similar situations do not necessarily exist elsewhere. In fact, it is probably quite common for a single practitioner to work on behalf of both   arties, or all three parties where a love triangle is involved. Some of the practitioners interviewed for this book admitted to "playing both sides," so to speak, although they did not wish to be identified as doing so. Most businesses involve playing parties off against one another, and conjuring is a business just like any other. If the customer wants something and is willing to pay for it, these practitioners see no ethical or moral taboos against providing it, particularly in such morally gray areas as male-female relationships.

Use of head and pubic hair is common in love- and sex-oriented conjure. Mrs. S. in Charleston related the following prescriptions for keeping a man:

§§   Take two strands of your own hair and tie them together with two strands of his. Put them in a bottle of Hearts Cologne and add some Adam and Eve root. Every morning before your husband awakens, run water over the bottle for nine seconds, then daub some of the potion under your arms. Your man will stay close to you.

§§   Cut some of the hair from your left armpit and some from the right side of your groin. Burn the hair and while doing so make the wish that you want your husband to be true to you. Pound the ashes into a fine dust and serve it to him in his food.

§§   Obtain some of the man's hair—from his head, from under his arms, and from his pubic area. Wrap the hair in one of his soiled black socks and boil it. Put some pins and some black pepper in the sock and bury it in the ground, under the doorstep or under the house. The sock will draw him to you and he will think of you more than of any other woman.

Urine and menstrual blood are also used, although, my sources assure me, such ingredients are used less frequently than more mundane items like hair or pieces of clothing. Mother K. in the Louisville area gave the following prescriptions:

§§   To keep a man crazy about her and uninterested in wandering, a woman simply has to mix some of her menstrual blood into his food or drink.

§§   Also to keep a man true, scrub your porch with your urine (the older term commonly used was chamber lye), lime, and sugar. Wash his socks and rinse them in your urine before hanging them out to dry.

§§   A third prescription is to take the man's urine and put it in a bottle with two tablespoons full of sugar. Bury the vial under the front porch or steps.

The association between excretory and sexual functions is a common and traditional one. Many of the formulas for keeping a man at home involve "stopping up" his urine. My informants supplied the following prescriptions for bringing about such discomfort:

§§   Take some of his urine and put it into a bottle with some sugar and some pure, sweet milk—ideally, fresh from a cow. Cap the bottle tightly and upend it and place it on the floor under or near your bed. If you are feeling particularly diabolical, you can bury the bottle or otherwise hide it away, and eventually the man will blow up!

§§   A simpler method is to place his urine alone in a bottle and stop it up tight. He will stay "stopped up" as long as the bottle does, or until it kills him.

Another common body of prescriptions for keeping a man true involves keeping a portion of his semen in order to "take his nature" from him. The persons I interviewed differed among themselves as to whether or not such prescriptions prevented a man from ejaculating at all or simply from ejaculating with any woman but the one who captured his "nature." At any rate, here are some methods of taking a man's "nature."

§§ According to a New Orleans practitioner, you must take a dish rag to bed with you and sleep with it under your pillow for three nights, burning a white candle each of the three days from noon to one p.m. On the fourth night, after intercourse, use the dish rag with your husband in place of a towel. Thereafter, he will be unable to have intercourse with anyone but you.

§§ A similar prescription from Mother K. in Louisville substitutes a dish towel and dispenses with the candle ritual.

§§ Mrs. S. in Charleston provided a more diabolical prescription, also using a cloth on which a man has wiped himself. The cloth is then put in a bottle and buried, depriving him of his "nature" entirely. And if the bottle is buried upside down, his semen will go to his head and cause his death.

One of the oldest and most common methods of keeping a man true is the "nine knots" method, some version of which most of my sources offered:

§§ While your husband is sleeping, take a piece of thread or string and measure the length of his penis. Tie nine knots in the string or thread and wear it at your waist.

§§ Purchase a length of yellow cloth and take it to bed when you and your husband plan to have intercourse. Make sure some of his discharge gets on the cloth. Tear a thin strip from the cloth and knot it nine times, cursing other women as you tie each knot. Wear it at your waist or otherwise close to your body. Save the rest of the cloth and take it to bed every night and your husband will be unable to have sex with another woman.

King Solomon's Guide also has a prescription for keeping a man home at night, although it is one of the more costly. Ingredients amounted to $15.32 at this writing.

§§ 2 Drive Away Evil incense and oil
    2 Compelling Power incense and oil
      Uncrossing Power incense and oil
    2 Strong Love cologne
    2 Seven Holy Spirits bath oil
    2 Make Your Wish sand

Mix Drive Away Evil, Compelling incense and Uncrossing incense together. Burn each day until all incenses are used. Anoint your body with the Compelling oil. Throw a little Make Your Wish sand toward the east for nine mornings before sunrise. Take seven baths with Seven Holy Spirits bath oil. Put Strong Love cologne behind your ears when you are near him.

§§§   **How A Man Can Escape**

Lest it appear to the reader, particularly the male reader, that the hapless husband is doomed to a life without his "nature" or one of involuntary sexual loyalty, there are several methods he can employ to get his "nature" back or escape his wife's power.

§§ **An initiate in Birmingham prepares a special bath powder which the man must mix with water and wash in the new moon on three alternate nights. She would not reveal the ingredients of the powder but did say she purchased them from a mail-order house.**

§§ **Mother K. in Louisville prescribes an antidote made from blue grass. Boil about a pound of the grass and drain the grass from the "pot liquor." Let the liquid stand for twenty-four hours, then drink nine swallows on each of the next six mornings. By the seventh morning the man's nature will have returned.**

Two prescriptions, both given by male practitioners, involve the same item the woman uses to take the man's nature from him, a dish rag:

§§ **Steal a dish rag—any dish rag, not necessarily one that belongs to, or has been used by, the woman—wash well and frequently with it and eventually your nature will come back.**

§§   Take an old greasy dish rag and wash yourself with it every day for seven days. Hide it between washings so no one else will touch it or use it for anything else.

Here are three more prescriptions supplied by various practitioners:

§§   You must find a young girl who has not yet menstruated but who is in her teens and obtain some of her urine. Mix it with saltpeter and take it as medicine.

§§   Take two red onions and squeeze them into a brand new handkerchief. Then dip the handkerchief into spirits of turpentine. Wash the penis with the handkerchief.

§§   Bathe in jimson weed (a narcotic) and saltpeter three times a day for nine days. Unfortunately, this is not guaranteed to cure impotency, but it will ease the condition somewhat.

The Lucky Starr Products Company in Columbus, Georgia, sells Pucoon Root in Liquid, an "Old Indian Cure for Lost Nature," that costs $7.00 for a four-ounce bottle.

Relatively simple spells are undone with relative ease. When spells involve things that are hidden, for example, it is necessary only to find the hiding place and remove the item.

§§ Take nine swallows of water and you will be able to go right to the hiding place and pick up whatever it is that is tying you down.

If a belt tied around a tree is "tying you down," you must find the belt and remove it. If your woman has buried the dry skin of your heel to keep you at home, you must find where she has buried it. But generally you need a hoodoo practitioner to tell you what is tying you down and where it is hidden.

§§§ How a Woman Makes Her Husband Sleep

Most of the practitioners interviewed for this book indicated that their major business came from women seeking to keep their men true in one way or another, but there is a smaller body of practices concerned with unfaithful women. There are methods to make a man sleep so the woman might "step out"—methods usually not needed by men, who have traditionally had more freedom to go outside the home. Since women have had fewer reasons to leave home and hearth, they have found it necessary to employ potions and prescriptions to cause their husbands to sleep. Following are some such prescriptions:

§§ In New Orleans the woman is likely to use candles for this purpose. She writes his name on each of two slow-burning candles, one pink and one green, waits until he is asleep and lights them just before she goes out. As soon as they burn down the man will wake up, but they should be the kind that burn five to six hours, giving her ample time.

Other methods use the principle of like-to-like.

§§ The woman waits until the man is asleep, then spreads her panties over his face and walks backwards out of the room. Or she waits until he's asleep and then turns his shoe soles up and crosses them under the bed. For extra protection both methods may be employed.

§§ She may also have intercourse with him, wait until he is asleep, and then take a piece of her underwear and a piece of his, wrap them tightly together and place them somewhere around the bed—under the mattress, for example. He will stay tied to the bed as long as the garments are there.

To run around a woman need not necessarily cause deep sleep in her man. A woman with a naive and unsuspecting husband can obtain a long period of freedom if she can get him to wear, even for an hour, a pair of shoes or boots into which she has placed small bags of roots. It might be added that any man who would put on footwear containing such items just because his wife said they would not harm him and in fact would be good for him probably deserves to be cheated on!

§§§   To Keep a Woman Home

Naturally the husband has recourse against such wifely machinations. The nine-knot method is applicable here, according to Dr. T. in New Orleans:

§§   The man must take a strap from one of her brassieres or slips. For nine nights he ties one knot in the strap and carries it with him in his pocket, thereby tying her to him and preventing her from running around on him.

§§   A woman can be deprived of her "nature" in ways similar to those by which a man's "nature" is taken from him. After having intercourse with her the husband wipes himself with a new handkerchief, places it in a bottle and stops it up. As long as the bottle is undisturbed, she will have no sexual feeling.

§§   Silver dimes can also be used to cut off a woman's nature (or a man's nature for that matter). The man, in this case, obtains a freshly worn pair of the woman's panties and cuts from the inside of the seat a piece about the size of a silver dollar. In it he wraps five new dimes, the silver of which sticks to the mucous or discharge. Carried in the man's pocket, the cloth and dimes become a "hand" that keeps the woman sexually inactive.

§§   A rather oddly simple method is used in New Orleans to keep a woman home. As women are associated with the hearth, the man need only take a hammer and drive two small nails into it to keep his woman by it.

§§   And finally, Dr. Sam reported a rather bizarre punishment for teaching a sexually disloyal woman the error of her ways. Take a toad and whip it with two sticks until it rears up on its hind legs. Put him in a pan of hot, fresh grease and fry him. Remove toad from pan and allow grease to cool. Next time sex is had with the woman, rub some of the salve inside her. Once it is inside her, any man who enters her will get stuck.

§§§   How a Woman Escapes

In order to get such "tricks" off, the woman has recourse similar to a man's. She may obtain a special bath potion from a root worker or practitioner, locate whatever is tying her down—e.g., the nails in the hearth—and remove it. Or, according to Mrs. M. in Montgomery, she can cause the man to lose whatever "mojo" or "hand" he is carrying against her.

§§   Obtain some fresh peppermint leaves and rub them in your hands and go back and fondle your husband. He will lose the "hand" from his pocket.

§§§   To Bring a Loved One Back

Another relatively substantial body of practices
is aimed at bringing back a loved one who has
deserted. Most of these rituals and potions are
for the purpose of helping a woman get back
her man. Several involve the use of a photograph or the writing of the person's name.

§§   **Take his picture and with four pins pin it facing
against the back of the headboard, so the face looks
"through the headboard" at the sleeper. That will fix
his mind on you.**

§§   **Take his or her photograph and place it face
down on a table. Place a red candle on top of it.
Burn red candles on it three hours in the evening
and three hours in the morning for six days. Turn
the picture face up and continue the candle burning
ritual for three more days. This will bring the person
back.**

§§   **Take the man's photograph and place it over
the top of a small glass of water and put the glass
under your bed. That will bring him back across the
water to your bed.**

§§   **After sunset write the man's name on each of
four pieces of paper at the four corners of the house.
Put the pieces of paper under your pillow before
you go to bed. Every night for eight nights thereafter, write his name on each of the four pieces of**

paper at each of the four corners of the house and sleep on them. He will come back.

§§ Write his name nine times on a piece of paper. Place the paper under a glass or jar of oil and burn floating wicks in the oil for nine nights.

Other practices make use of a garment belonging to the absent person and the principle of like-to-like:

§§ Take an article of his clothing to the graveyard and bury it in a grave. Ask the spirit in the grave to help bring the man back. Leave it there for three days. On the evening of the third day, return to the grave and remove the item and a small portion of the dirt from the grave. Add salt to that and put all three things above the door by which he left. In nine days he will return.

§§ Take an article of his clothing and walk three steps backwards out your door. Dig a hole and bury the item, praying to God to bring the man back.

§§ Obtain a dirt dauber's nest. Cut up an article of the man's clothing and stop up the holes in the nest with small pieces of the cloth. This will cause the man to return.

Other methods for bringing a man back home are these:

§§ Burn goofer dust with sugar and a little bit of salt and make your wish. (Goofer dust is available at hoodoo supply houses. Some sources liken it to mere anvil dust. Others say it is a mixture of grave yard dust, salt and brimstone, and still others say it is powdered dry rattlesnake head and graveyard dust.)

§§ Put red pepper and guinea seeds in a small piece of his favorite meat. Bury it by your door exactly at noon or exactly at six (mealtimes) and in three days he will be back (assuming he likes your cooking.)

§§§ To Break Up a Couple.

There are many other prescriptions employed by men and women against each other or for or against couples. Suppose a woman wishes to break up a couple (females seem to be the chief villains in this area). These are some of the methods she can employ:

§§ Take anvil dust and place it on a tray or in a small kettle with a piece of paper on which the couple's name has been written. Wait until the dark of the moon and burn the two items stirring them and chanting, "Break up this home." Do this every other night until the moon gets light. By that time the couple will be quarreling. Repeat the process at the next dark of the moon and by the time the moon gets light the second time the relationship will be over.

§§ Get a cat and a dog and cause them to bristle at each other. While they are bristling, cut some of the hair of each, put it in a small box, seal it tightly, and shake it vigorously for nine mornings. The couple will begin fighting "like cats and dogs."

§§ Take an egg, preferably from a mockingbird's nest, although some informants say the eggs of other small birds will do. Go to the couple's home and break the egg in a corner of the house. That will break the peace in the house and the couple will separate.

§§§ How a Couple Ensures Unity

Perhaps the couple does not wish to separate. Several sources suggested the tying of a "love knot." One partner, usually the man, takes a handkerchief and ties two knots in it. The woman in turn ties two knots in it. Then the four knots are tied together into one knot and both man and woman pull to make the knot so tight that no one can untie it. Another method, used by a practitioner in New Orleans when an endangered couple seeks her help, is to take some Valentine Incense and "dress" or anoint a candle with it. Burn the candle in a mixture of sugar and perfume.

§§§ To Keep Another Man/Woman Away From Your Woman/Man

Mother W. offered this method, which uses a homemade "Stay Away" potion:

§§ **Take equal parts of crushed John the Conqueror root, lodestone, and sassafras. Crush them into a powder and sprinkle the powder into the drinking water of the person to be affected, that is, the one who poses the threat.**

And of course, hoodoo does not neglect to address the age-old mother-in-law problem. *King Solomon's Alledged Guide to Success? Power!* gives the following prescription for getting rid of such an evil influence. Total cost of ingredients at the Dixie Drug Store: $14.01.

§§ **3 Drive Away Evil incense**
2 Drive Away Evil oil
3 Jinx Killer incense
1 Jinx Killer oil
2 Indian Spray
2 Angel Sand

§§ **Mix one tablespoon full of Drive Away Evil oil and Jinx Killer oil and pour on incenses as they burn. Spray the house regularly with Indian Spray. Sprinkle Angel Sand around the home and you will see a change in one month. To be safe, spray the house with Indian Spray once a week thereafter.**

VIII

Voodoo and Hoodoo
in Perspective

You've seen quite a few conjure recipes in the
last four chapters, recipes covering most major
aspects of life. Understand though that black
people, even when most believed in the power
of voodoo and hoodoo, weren't unduly fatalis-
tic about their chances of making it through life
without being infested with snakes, or stricken
ill through unnatural means, "tied" by their
spouses, or made to leave town against their
will. Throughout the history of voodoo and
hoodoo people have been comforted by knowing that they retained an element of control
over any threatening forces. There's no charm
that can't be broken; one needs only to find a
practitioner who has a sufficiently powerful
prescription to break it. Popular white mythology notwithstanding (the blacks' inordinate
fright at seeing the white-robed and -hooded
Klansmen in D. W. Griffiths' "The Birth of a
Nation" comes to mind), blacks have never
feared either magic or the supernatural. They
have feared only what could be done to harm
them using magic or with the help of the
supernatural. Black slaves were not especially

preoccupied with the danger of conjure any more than their masters lived in constant fear that their wives would die in childbirth, or than most of us go around worrying that we will be run over by an automobile. Voodoo and hoodoo served an important socially cohesive function for blacks and acted as a major vehicle in the preservation of the African heritage. However, the need it has served for the past few centuries is no longer as important as it once was, and there is some question whether it will continue to survive as a distinct black cultural phenomenon.

Voodoo and hoodoo in the New World have never constituted a well-integrated system of belief and practice. For a long time there has been too much distance, both geographical and chronological, from the roots in Africa. There has been too much cross-cultural contact and influence, too much distortion of values and modes of expression. But the disintegrative process is accelerating. Voodoo and hoodoo are being eroded at both ends, so to speak, not just through declining interest on the part of many blacks but through increased self-interest on the part of many blacks as well, not just through humorous skepticism on the part of some whites but also through the increased inclination of other whites to practice formerly black forms of spiritualism.

Sensing the erosion of even the purer aspects of voodoo and hoodoo, some blacks have taken steps to return to the African mystical-magical roots. One area where this attempt has been made is Oyotunji, South Carolina, the only village in North America devoted to perpetuating the language, dress, customs, and living

conditions of the Yoruba. Founded in 1969 by
Walter Serge King, who has taken the name
Oba (King) Afuntola, the village proclaims itself
as "the only village in North America built by
priests of the Orisha-Voodoo gods," and indeed
the practice of voodoo is among the most well
known of its customs. For awhile the village
acted as a center of voodoo practice and
attracted considerable business. Afuntola's
wives were among the chief practitioners, and
they spoke openly to visitors of their malefic
conjure and of their willingness to kill for a
price. Had they continued their voodoo enterprise, they might have made the village the
richest in North America.

By 1975, however, the inhabitants of
Oyotunji had gone out of the malefic conjure
business. The demand for evil "tricks" had
been so great that it was almost impossible to
meet. And strange ills had begun to befall the
village—animals died, people got sick, legal
authorities became concerned and nosy, and
there was strife among the villagers. Nowadays
only the more benign forms of voodoo are
practiced, such as readings and divination.

Priests will look into the future, prescribe
sacrifices to prevent illness, or provide potions
to bring back a lover. Simple readings cost
$5.00; love potions $25.00 a quart; and prices for
the performance of sacrifices range from $25.00
to well over $100.00. At Oyotunji, a well-heeled
client can even "buy" a voodoo god: Elegba
costs $120.00; Orosun, god of fortune-telling,
goes for $200.00. The price includes the animals
needed for the sacrifice and a pot in which the
god is supposed to reside.

The people of Oyotunji are probably not

trying to swindle the public with their voodoo business. This is not the case with some others. According to the people I interviewed, the number of bogus "doctors" is on the increase, and since they have access through the commercial hoodoo supply houses to the same ingredients as legitimate practitioners, it is difficult for the layman to tell the difference.

While we are on the subject of the merchandise sold by the hoodoo and spiritualist supply houses, it should be noted that many of the most powerful-sounding items are actually harmless home concoctions not worth their high prices. Ingredients vary depending on the supplier, of course, but Fast Luck Water is likely to be ordinary water colored with Easter egg dyes; War Water, oil of tar in water; Van-Van Oil, lemon juice and wood alcohol; Black Cat Oil, common machine oil darkened with dye; Flying Devil Oil, a mixture of olive oil and red pepper; Move Quick Powder, a combination of cinnamon, red pepper, and confectioners sugar, Drawing Powder, mere confectioners sugar, and so on.

Also, there appears to be an increased tendency on the part of properly trained and otherwise legitimate practitioners to engage in some rather questionable methods.

Not that the ethics of hoodoos have traditionally been above reproach. The Hampton Institute students reported some evidence of shady practice back in the 1890s. To quote Herron's and Bacon's article:

... as a rule, before he does anything for the patient (the conjure-doctor) demands and receives a large fee. Should he find business slack he will sometimes take it upon himself to secure patients by visiting certain persons and telling them that they have been or are about to be conjured, and often preventing irrefragable proofs in the shape of a pin stuck in the north side of a distant tree, or a bottle dug up at a certain designated spot in the yard. He exacts a payment of money for his services in preventing the evil sure to follow if he is not engaged by a good-sized retainer to prevent it.

Some practitioners seem willing to cooperate with each other at the expense of their clients. It is possible, of course, that this is not a new development. A certain amount of such cooperation may have taken place among the practitioners of whom I knew as a child, for example. On occasion I heard mutterings in the community that Dr. X. and Mrs. Y. seemed awfully friendly for competitors, but in retrospect I do not believe they were sufficiently astute to engage in, for example, price-fixing. Nowadays practitioners are more likely to be in cahoots with each other. According to one reliable source, an interesting partnership exists between a female practitioner in a small town in Mississippi and a male practitioner in Jackson. Her trade is mostly women and comprises primarily conjure aimed at keeping their men true. His practice is chiefly lifting the spells from the husbands. She puts the spells on for $25 and he removes them for $75. She receives her kickback in the form of free hoodoo supplies. And how is that for American free enterprise?

Practitioners' services were never free, but their rates used to be more reasonable. One nonpractitioner suggested facetiously that perhaps medical conjure ought to be brought under the auspices of Medicaid. Rising fees are contributing to the corresponding rise in do-it-yourself spiritualism and conjure. "Most people are learning now to do it themselves, because spiritualists charge quite a lot," says Joseph Bush. "For some spiritualists it's a real racket." Frank Hendricks estimates that sometimes they get 50-100 customers buying spiritualist supplies at the Dixie Drug Store a day, of whom sixty percent are individual users and forty percent are spiritualists. These individual users learn by means of the various how-to books and pamphlets that proliferate on the market, but they are not always successful. "There was this lady from Mississippi," Hendricks recalled. "She came in every two weeks for three years to purchase different items to solve her own problem. Eventually she admitted she'd had very little success. I gave her the names of three spiritualists. In two weeks one of them had accomplished what she had been unable to do herself. She came back to tell me about it."

Even do-it-yourself hoodoo and voodoo can be expensive to practice, as indicated by the prices of the ingredients needed for the recipes in *King Solomon's Alledged Guide to Success? Power!* and by the prices of Mr. Felix's gambling hands. Blacks' financial condition may have improved in the last two decades, but in order for hoodoo and spiritualist suppliers to charge such prices at least a portion of their clientele must be white. Actually the existence of white believers in black spiritualism is not a new phenomenon. There were one or two practitioners in this author's Alabama town who had some white clients, primarily from out of state. "We have as many white customers here as we have black," says Joseph Bush of the Dixie Drug Store. "Whites might send blacks in to buy the stuff for them, but as far as usage, it's about on an even basis." One of my sources has a white husband. According to a neighbor, he does not try to prevent his wife from practicing, "because he's under the stuff himself. He can't help himself. . . . I think he might suspect he's under a spell, but he doesn't say anything about it. He stays right around the house with her, don't go out, like a man should, like a normal man. He gotta believe in that stuff, else he'd act more normal."

There are voodoo and hoodoo purists—actually a contradiction in terms given the acknowledged cultural impurity of the art—who decry this increased white presence and participation in what has traditionally been a primarily black domain, predicting that it will further dilute, and eventually bring about the demise of, that aspect of the black cultural heritage. Their regret is understandable. It is lamentable that future generations of black youngsters will not hear stories like the ones I heard from Grandma Hattie. But black Americans cannot have it both ways. The more access they have to mainstream American life the more their unique traditions will be subsumed into mainstream American traditions. Actually it is doubtful that voodoo and hoodoo will ever die out altogether. Whenever earthly, secular, non-mystical life becomes too hard to handle, whenever social upheaval occurs, whenever religion and mysticism enjoy a renaissance, voodoo and hoodoo will re-emerge as well, if indeed they are ever fully eclipsed. Historically they have not known the ups and downs of popularity that have plagued European witchcraft or spiritualism, and they may well continue to be celebrated as part of a long, mostly proud heritage by blacks and respected for their tenacity by whites. They may come to include other cultural elements, and be buffeted about in the storms of changing mores, but, like the people whom they have nurtured for centuries, they will have survived, and that in itself is a victory.

Bibliography

Barrett, Leonard E. *Soul-Force: African Heritage in Afro-American Religion.* Garden City, N.Y.: Doubleday, 1974.

Brewer, J. Mason. *American Negro Folklore.* New York: Quadrangle, 1974

Coon, Nelson. *Using Plants for Healing.* New York: Hearthside Press, Inc., 1963

Elworthy, Frederick. *The Evil Eye.* New York: Gordon Press, 1970.

Hall, Julien A. "Negro Conjuring and Tricking," *Journal of American Folk-Lore,* Vol. 10 (1897), 241-243.

Haskins, James. *Witchcraft, Mysticism and Magic in the Black World.* Garden City, N.Y.; Doubleday, 1974.

Haskins, Jim, and Hugh F. Butts, M.D. *The Psychology of Black Language.* New York: Barnes and Noble, 1973.

Herron (Miss) and Miss A.M. Bacon. "Conjuring and Conjure-Doctors in the Southern United States," *Journal of American Folk-Lore,* Vol. 9 (1896), 143-147, 224-226.

Herskovits, Melville J. "African Gods and Catholic Saints in New World Negro Belief," *American Anthropologist,* Vol. 39 (1937), 635-643.

———. *The Myth of the Negro Past*. Boston: Beacon Press, 1958.

Hughes, Langston, and Arna Bontemps, eds. *The Book of Negro Folklore*. New York: Dodd Mead, 1958.

Hurston, Zora Neale. "Hoodoo in America," *Journal of American Folk-Lore*, Vol. 44 (1931), 317-417.

———. *Mules and Men*. Westport, Conn.: Negro Universities Press, repr. of 1935 ed.

Middleton, John, ed. *Gods and Rituals*. Austin, Tex.: University of Texas Press, 1976.

———. *Magic, Witchcraft, and Curing*. Austin, Tex.: University of Texas Press, 1976.

Moore, (Miss) Ruby Andrews. "Superstitions of Georgia." *Journal of American Folk-Lore*, Vol. 5 (1892), 230-231; Vol. 9 (1896), 227-228.

Parrinder, Geoffrey. *Witchcraft: European and African*. London, 1963.

Pendleton, Louis. "Negro Folk-Lore and Witchcraft in the South," *Journal of American Folk-Lore*, Vol. 3 (1890), 201-207.

Puckett, Newbell N. *Folk Beliefs of the Southern Negro*. Westport, Conn.: Greenwood Press, repr. of 1926 ed.

———. "Religious Folk-Beliefs of Whites and Negroes," *Journal of Negro History*, Vol. 16 (1931), 9-35.

Tallant, Robert. *Voodoo in New Orleans*. New York: Macmillan, 1962.

Turner, Victor. *The Forest of Symbols: Aspects of Ndembu Ritual*. Ithaca, N.Y.: Cornell University Press, 1967.

§§

Index

Index